Discover Your Power Quotient

(A Modern *Arthasastra* for those Who Want to be Powerful)

Y. S. Rajan

rajpal

Price : ₹ 125 (Rupees One Hundred Twenty Five only)

ISBN : 978-81-7028-850-3

1st Published 2010
2nd Printing 2011
DISCOVER YOUR POWER QUOTIENT : Modern *Arthasastra* for Those Who Want to be Powerful by *Y.S.Rajan*
Printed at Anand Son's, Delhi

RAJPAL & SONS, Kashmere Gate, Delhi-110 006
website : www.rajpalpublishing.com
e-mail : mail@rajpalpublishing.com

Contents

Preface — *v*

Section-I

Chapter 1

Recent Past to the Present: Changes in Attitudes — 3

Chapter 2

Power Aspirations among Different Groups of Indian Youth — 7

Chapter 3

Various Facets of Power Quotient — 11

- Political Power — 11
- Money Power — 14
- Crime Power — 17
- Media Power — 20
- State Power — 24
- Mass Entertainment Power — 27
- Emotion Power — 33
- Backroom Power — 36

Chapter 4

What is the Modern *Arthasastra*? 38

– Knowledge Power 42

– Moral Power 43

Chapter 5

Epilogue to the First Section 45

Section-II

Chapter 6

Practical Considerations for Entering Power Structures 49

– Political Power 53

– Money Power 57

– Crime Power 61

– Media Power 64

– State Power 69

– Mass Entertainment Power 74

– Emotion Power 78

– Backroom Power 80

– Knowledge Power 83

– Moral Power 85

Chapter 7

How to Assess Your Power Quotient (PQ) 87

Preface

This book has been written after a lot of careful thought. The book was in "my mind" for several years and crystallized during 2008. The final shape, after several iterations, took place during October 2008. The publication comes after the momentous general election to the Lok Sabha and a few state assemblies (2009). In many ways the election is the reflection of people's angst and aspirations, and their dreams and desires. People allow for a lot of leeway to the politicians (those on the top of the power—a point hierarchy of Indian society) but there is a self-limiting brake put on them beyond a point. That point is difficult to determine *a priori*. It is clear that all the predictions by electoral *pundits* and media hypes, have gone wrong consistently during 2004, 2009 and also in other major elections in between.

Does it mean that the power quotient (PQ) of people in India has changed dramatically? The answer is an emphatic "No!" Dynasties remain and in fact, they have spread to every party and every group. It is now accepted as natural. Money power has also played a major role. But its dependence on politics was remarkably demonstrated by the explosive shooting up of the Sensex after the 2009 election. Though the

Election Commission did a remarkable job by formulating certain rules and guidelines to check the entrance of the tainted people in politics, only a naive person can say that crime power did not play a role, for all parties. Many eminent achievers who stood as independents were trounced! Media continued doing various forms of influence peddling though exit polls were banned by the Election Commission. While their overall predictions were wrong, in a number of cases, media could influence the course of events; it showed its power.

The above recapitulations are done only to emphasise the fact that what is written in this book, is quite relevant and reflective of the present scenario. Yes, the Indian power structure as it stands now, has evolved over many centuries and adapted itself to the new processes of constitutional democracy, modern administrative and business systems. But to claim that we have achieved equality and equity, will only be cheating ourselves. Statements such as "Any Indian boy or girl should aspire to become big and powerful; if they dream, or make a firm resolve to achieve or just work hard to realize the goal of becoming successful and powerful" are only meant to deceive a vast majority of ordinary people of adults, if they are not tempered with identification of certain harsh realities along with specific suggestions which can help to progress even amidst these difficult situations.

I still stand for ideals, scientific, rational thinking, ethics, morals and an inclusiveness which extend beyond humanism to everything in nature, and try to stand by these principles to the best extent possible in my private and public life. But I have come to realize for the past many years, say over one and half decade or more, that it will not be correct to pass them on in an unmixed form or without caveats to the younger generation. Of course, they will discover the untenability or even non-existence of many cliched "imaginary" realities of ideal life. But many of them may be seriously hurt in the process, often irreversibly.

I continuously learn from interacting with people, talking and listening to them, observing them and empathizing with them. I travel extensively to all parts of India. I realize that there are many persons (especially the younger ones) who do not want to accept the possibility of tempering themselves with a middle path even if it were to be discovered by themselves. They desire to be powerful and influential. They have sharp PQ. Perhaps it is a part of the natural wired instinct derived over millions of years of evolution from amoeba to the current form.

A quotation from evolutionary theorists E.O. Wilson and David Sloan Wilson will be worth noting:

> "Selfishness beats altruism within groups. Altruistic groups beat selfish groups"*
>
> One of the powerful hymn from the *Atharvaveda* says:
>
> "Bhuyema Sharadahshadam"
>
> "May we retain our prestige and influence for hundred years" (4966, *Atharvaveda*, LX VIII)

The desire to be powerful and influential is also considered a rightful part of the prayer.

And above all, let us not forget the great Indian heritage of *Arthasastra*. That was an important part of the learning by the kings, ministers, rulers, aspirants for the kingdom, etc. It is a part of the *aparavidya*, education in the temporal world. The Indian great epic *Mahabharata* is full of power plays,

---

* *Scientific American India*, January 2009, P. 27, What is Good of the Group of Steve Mirsky.

politics, ego trips, intrigues, etc. along with many excellent examples of virtues, as well. A judicious mix of altruism and selfishness is apparently a part of nature's evolution.

Thus after a lot of thinking, I decided that it is essential to expose to the young people, many realities of power plays and power hierarchies as they exist in societies, especially in the Indian context in the beginning of 21st century. This book can be considered as a modern *Arthasastra*. It is to guide those who aspire for power or are passionate about their own personal power or are keenly looking for opportunities to make proper use of their PQ. It exposes them to the stark realities of how the power terrain is now and would perhaps be for several decades to come. Those who aspire for it should know the truths. It is not to scare any one nor to be cynical about how things are. It is to see one's environment clearly and with a sharper eyes for the preys and predators, since the aspirant is likely to face a tough ride.

An innovation in this book is to articulate on the existing layers of power. Political power will always be at the top though its "height" may vary. Knowing about several levels will help the aspirant to choose a realistic level to try for. It is for setting goals for themselves. That is the reason Section-II of the book elaborates on how an individual can identify her/his real motivations and then choose the path to power. Every effort in life requires a price to be paid. A person wanting to become a great ascetic has to be prepared to lose all other enjoyments. A person pursuing a difficult scientific research may have limited family life and may lose many promotions, but may end up with great awards. Similar will be the lifestyle for those pursuing other levels of power hierarchies. The physical, external and internal (one's own) constraints are spelt out as questions to be answered by the aspirant.

In the past the *Arthasastra* and similar such writings

quoted therein, were kept secret. The power games were secret "palace politics". Despite remnants of various forms of old feudalism, colonialism, and other forms of exclusive power mongering extremisms, the 21st century has a much greater democratic participation in the power games. In that sense, many ordinary men and women not born within the privileged families of existing power hierarchies (political, money, even crime (!), media, state power, etc. outlined in this book), can also aspire for power and be able to succeed. But not just with an aspiration for an amorphous entity called power. Active practitioners of power games and especially those who have been successfully rewarded, will make statements which will create an impression in other (often naive) aspirants that it is all due to lots of sincere hard work by them! They won't even say "with a bit of luck!" Nobody in the upper decks of power-hierarchy will help a person from below to climb up! They may use others as ladders for their own rise, but will not give a helping hand. That is the very nature of power games.

But the simple formula of "hard work" and "single-minded vision and goal" will not work. Most of the people who are now powerful and have become icons have smartly played their "power games" which have a different set of rules, ethics, etc.! Not the popular versions of value systems which are being preached for the bulk of the pliant masses and youth! If aspirants for power live according to the preached value systems and work hard, they are likely to be knocked out midway. They will be exploited by those who are ahead and also by their competitors who will knock them out midway. The classical *Arthasastra* describes how the relatives of the kings (starting from their brothers and sons) are the worst enemies to be watched out.

In the power systems of today which are accessible to more persons, there are few "friends" and more "enemies" everywhere. The degrees of cunning and ruthlessness required to eliminate "enemies" and acquire new "friends" are crucial power games in the 21st century society particularly in India. Even for getting into powerful positions within Government science labs, universities or corporate world or media, such skills of eliminating enemies (with or without new alliances) are crucial.

This book brings out the realities of present society and salient features of methodologies required for such power in the open, so that the aspirants who are large in number (and who will continue to increase because of the huge young and growing population in India) can chalk out their plans to reach higher in the hierarchy of power.

Also they can find a suitable (and viable as judged at the time of starting) level of the power hierarchy to aspire for or to work for to begin with so that their risks are minimized and chances of success are increased. Also they can customize the paths to suit their own PQ and the constraints they are most likely to face.

The questions posed for each of the power hierarchy in Section-II have several sets of answers. There is nothing called final answer to these. They can be debated in your mind. The idea is to develop, in the reader, a feeling of informed clarity. Finally, a sprint race of marathon is to be run by the athlete. Honing of various skills including well-being of different critical parts of the body is important for the athlete. But it is the athlete's attitude that is more important. That is why there are many questions which allow the reader to judge their own attitudes towards various power games.

It is in the sense of bringing more persons into the modern power games, this book attempts to do which can claim to draw inspiration from *Arthasastra* in the modern 21st century context. Hopefully, it can strengthen the process of democratization by enabling many more ordinary persons to play the power games effectively and thus realise their aspirations to be powerful and influential.

I believe when more and more people participate in the power games, thus breaking the exclusive prerogative of a few ruling classes (as it exists now because of the knowledge asymmetry between those in power and bulk of ordinary naive citizens and aspirants), world will have a chance of becoming a more equitable place. At that time, many persons will volitionally move towards moral power which in the present time, has become an utopian concept or hope.

It is with this innate democratic aspiration, I have attempted to present this book to the readers.

I wish them all good luck to realize success in the power games they chart out for themselves.

Vijayee Bhavah!

Y.S. Rajan

SECTION – I

Power will intoxicate the best hearts, as wine the strongest heads. No man is wise enough nor good enough to be trusted with unlimited power.

– Walter Colton

Conceptual Framework and Practical Orientation

This section brings out the realities of hierarchies of power structures in world in general, and in India, in particular. Eight levels of power hierarchies are identified which will provide an understanding of the power quotient of people of different backgrounds and different age groups. It also gives tips for practical orientation for those who would like to enter into the level or rise up further in the levels and the associated risks are pointed out.

1

Recent Past to the Present Changes in Attitudes

When I was young during the 1950s, 1960s and 1970s, the dominating social themes in India were based on utopian idealism: Truth will win; hard work pays; as nation develops all Indians will benefit; equality in society can be achieved by developing the country with science and industry; Indian democracy will help even the ordinary person to become leaders; India should not align in big power fights. I guess that such euphoric idealism was the dominant theme in many developing countries, which obtained their independence during the same period.

But during the 1980s and 1990s such idealism started cracking even amongst the youth let alone the older (more mature?) persons (personally I was slow to accept such a change; I believe that the earlier idealism can still have a role). The slogan of *Mera Bharat Mahan* or later 'Shining India' or similar such slogans did not catch public attention. Often these slogans met with derisive laughter at the upper echelons and at the level of ordinary people though they were ritually touted everywhere. It was not so with *Garibi Hatao* earlier in 1970s or 'self-reliance' in 1960s or 1970s. There could have been some critical voices but the flow was in one direction: "Yes, we can do it in our own unique Indian way – also achieve equality" was the general feeling.

But if we check with present day youth especially the middle class youth from big cities, most of them are not carried away by single point or simple idealist slogans or idealist imageries. They do have their icons, celebrities, popular movies like "Chak de India" or "Rang de Basanti" but these all are some periodic outbursts of enthusiasm or just plain entertainment. I don't think most of such youth are carried away by any passionate calls or speeches to make India super-power. But deep in their subconscious, they like to be associated with the slogan of India—the super-power—because their own individual values go up in the global market; they can aspire for more income, they can have more global opportunities. Their attitude to India or such general slogans is largely based on enlightened self-interest. They may not mind voting through e-mails or SMSes, it is probably treated as fun. And it is also a hype which creates great visions of superiority. However, most of them are goal-oriented—at least want to think so—about their education and career. But still when I have interacted with many of them and asked them during interactive talks from a stage (with a few hundreds of students participating) a question "How many of you are confident about your future?" I have seen only small percentage of them raise their hands even after some repetitive asking. This is so in youths in smaller towns and in villages. Only exception I found so far was in a rural school in Chikballapur (near Bangalore), which I visited recently, where children from a few nearby rural schools also had attended.

Many persons in the age group of 50 years and more, often complain that our youths have become too much materialistic (They don't look at themselves. Their lifestyles!

Nor those who were idealistic in their youth, tell whatever happened to their idealistic dreams!). One fact may be that India is growing fast now. In addition, a few decades of experience of independent existence is available, spanning over about 3 to 4 generations of India. Therefore, the social themes are more sober (Earlier in the 1950s and even 1960s it was much easier to blame the colonial power and their loot for every lapse of ours!). Now the recent social memories remind everybody of the realities. Naturally our youth too get to know these through facts and fiction. They see corruption and organised crimes all round them. They note that the 'rags to riches' stories are not all one of simple case of idealism, but behind them are many true facts of corrupt and even criminal practices. In other words, they are also exposed to (facts and fictions of) cold realities of life in India.

Hence they tend to be more pragmatic towards life. Some of them also try 'short-cuts' to success—beauty, money, etc. Much of their energies are also spent in competitive examinations and preparations for them or in entertainment from TV channels or using new products which their parents would not have easily obtained in their childhood or youth (This applies to youth in towns and villages except perhaps those who are very deprived.).

One very positive development amidst these changes is the increasing number of girls going to school and entering higher education. They are very particular to score high marks. Almost all over India percentage of girls in the toppers' list are disproportionate to their actual numbers. They want to win their freedom. BPO, KPO industries have given women many new economic opportunities and freedom. Old timers often are jealous to see young women earning almost as much as they do when they are in their fifties. Many of them say that Indian culture is being spoiled. Some bad incidents are exaggerated. But women are undaunted and get into newer jobs as hostesses, in retail trade, sales, office and in many spheres. Young men are easily adjusting to the new role of women as colleagues, even superiors, as friends and as working wives.

In the lower economic strata in villages and in small towns also, there is an increasing realisation among the youth that they have to make themselves a better life as their age cohorts do in bigger cities. Many young boys and men leave the odd jobs as agricultural labourers or even get away from their fathers' small land holdings to seek avenues in cities. Right from Punjab to Bihar to south, I learn from farmers that young boys are no longer interested in the low income-yielding agriculture. Often women in villages take up these tasks as boys leave for towns when they reach 16-17 years of age. They don't mind the odd jobs in cities, as they are able to enjoy better things in life.

It is, of course, a different story with the youth born in super rich families (of business persons, politicians, traders, rich farmers, powerful administrators, some rich professionals, contractors, actors, media persons, etc.). They are confident because their parents will make a future for them. They are often sent to USA, UK, and other foreign countries, after 10 or 10+2 schooling as their parents can afford the cost of their education. They come back after obtaining foreign degrees and then inherit companies, colleges, political positions, etc. For them there is no special case of idealism as they are, right from their childhood, made to believe that they are different from the rest of Indians and are born to rule! Such youth will form a very small percentage of their age cohorts. But clearly, they are emerging as the ruling class of the future, with direct inheritance of power (You can see dynasties in every sector of Indian society and economy.).

2

Power Aspirations Among Different Groups of Indian Youth

About 70% of youth in India don't go past 8th standard in the poorly equipped schools which alone their parents can afford. These youth are made to believe at a young age that they are no good for studies and learning. They have to eke out their existence in all and sundry "unorganised sector" (In India, after Independence most government institutions and private sector companies, hired class IV employees as peons, *safaiwalas*, etc. There was some benefit of security. Now most of these tasks are outsourced from the organised sectors to "unorganised" contractors. Hence these school drop-outs can hardly hope for "organised" sector jobs which are only 6 per cent of total employment in India!).

Another 20 per cent of the youth belong to the category of 10th, 11th or 12th pass. They are somewhat better equipped at least in reading and writing. Still most of them will not easily get jobs in the organised sector or well paying job opportunities opened up by globalisation, liberalisation and knowledge economy. Most of these persons feel that they have outgrown villages and seek odd jobs in towns and cities – end up as drivers, mechanics, assistants in small shops, hotels, tour guides, etc.

Another 8 per cent have higher education, often not tuned to needs of newly growing Indian economy. Still many of them struggle to get jobs after learning some additional skills in computers; or as teachers, para medics, etc. Unemployed among them are high as they will not do odd jobs. Their parents sacrifice a lot to educate them and even get into debts.

About 2 per cent of the youth constitutes the higher professional groups. Their numbers are still large in absolute terms as the base of each age cohort is about 20 million. These persons will add about 0.4 million every year. They and some of 8 per cent graduates together will come to about 1.5 million who are aspiring for better jobs – are touted by us as a great human capital of India. The sufferings borne by their parents and guardians are large, even offsetting some of the pleasures of modern life (This applies to lower and middle-middle class.).

These 1.5 million persons (every year entering into various jobs) enjoy better pay and quality of life and aspire to go abroad for more earning. Each of them wants a better economic and social space for themselves.

The other 18.5 million youths (say aged 18 years and entering into earning situations every year) struggle to live and get a secure job opportunity, which is often a mirage. In fact many below that age group, say from 14–15 years onwards, are in search of jobs. They will be 18.5 million for each age group.

Thus all the youths (except the fortunate ones belonging to the rich and super rich and power-privileged category) struggle for a better life. They have very little time to think of their actions in a larger context of a society. Most of them feel that they are a speck in the ocean. Of course, when they get something better for living—better shoes, better clothes or food or a dance opportunity or a movie—they want to enjoy, whatever little they get.

I believe that their attitudes are not at all wrong. Let us be honest. What has the governance or society or the nation given to them? They face problems everywhere; they see severe shortage of seats in schools, colleges; they see corruption, they see that recommendations are required to get school admission at nursery or any other stage; jobs require influence "network"—"Sir can you please put in a word?"—is a standard request which most youths aspiring for a seat or a job (in Government or in private sector) put to you, if you are accessible. They are also aware of the difficulties faced by their parents.

Desire for Power

In spite of all these uncertainties (or rather certainty of an inferior life!) many of these youths have some lurking desire for "power", i.e. their power quotient (PQ) is high. They want to be known to all! They aspire to be an actor, leader, etc. Many are afraid to say it. "How to realise your dream?" is a big question before them after they say, "I want to be so and so!" Just to repeat the cliché that hardwork will lead them there, does not seem to match with reality! "Well, it is destiny!" may sound more truthful!

Well, I don't want to invoke the destiny factor and leave them there.

I believe that the aspirations of the youth for "power" is normal and legitimate. It should not be buried under some old idealistic sayings such as "Nation is bigger than individual", "Think what you can give to nation", "Do something for others, that gives you joy", "Work for the team and its cause – not think of yourself!".

Most of those, who tell you these, are sitting pretty in their own powerful positions and do very little to share their power and glory with others!

I have attempted to give some important practical tips and newer value systems to these youth in my book *A-Z for Success: A Comparison for Youth*. It was meant to make them bold and develop strategies within their constraints, and not to be caught up in old clichés.

In this relatively small book, I intend to explain especially to these youths and those who are genuinely interested in the intricacies and realities of "power structure" in human societies particularly in the Indian context. I leave it to them as to what levels of power structure they want to reach. It will also help them face the onslaught and tricks of those who are now in those power structures and the establishments which help to perpetuate them.

3

Various Facets of Power Quotient

Political Power

The most important facet of Power Quotient in India is the political power. Probably it will be so in other countries as well for many decades to come. In many developed small European countries, the political power is not very powerful, as it is so in big developed countries or most developing countries. In countries like Switzerland, Iceland, Sweden, Norway, Netherlands, Finland, etc. political positions have more or less become another profession. The politicians travel like anybody else or drive like others. Being in or out of power does not mean huge loss of status or quality of life. These countries have reached a high quality of life for all its people. Economic and social space available for most people are large enough to satisfy the aspirations of many of them.

In bigger developed countries like USA, France, UK, Germany and Japan while quality of life of most of the people is very high and economic and social space available to most of them is also large, political positions bring a special global attention. Whether one likes it or not, President of USA becomes number one amongst global political leaders. USA, France and UK also control international politics through UN

Security Council and their own military power. Most other countries depend upon them for their own military hardware know-how and technology. Their military budgets raised through taxes of their people are huge. They thus handle large sums of money whose accountability is not as visible as it is in making roads, dams or public health systems. This non-transparency gives the ruling persons enormous clout. In addition, such huge budgets are also huge contracts, which domestic and foreign business persons cannot afford to miss out! It may be free market forces elsewhere in their countries or in the world but the political decisions of those in higher echelons of political power are crucial for deciding whether they lose out on a big contract. Indirectly these defence purchases are associated with huge high tech jobs and hence offer well paying jobs. Besides, there is also a political connection. Powerful politicians tend to take these jobs to their constituencies. Hence the big leader can exercise power over them. Such is the power of the political power structure in big developed countries. This is likely to continue for several decades.

Coming now to the developing countries where the political power is that of the highest sought-after level. In such countries poverty levels are very high. Middle classes are small—often struggling to live. Rich persons are a few percentage of the total. Therefore, public sector is large. Also most of these countries became independent around the middle of the twentieth century and adopted the centralised socialist policies, which concentrated the power in the political masters under the guise of or in the name of ruling for the people. For example, big public sector companies are "owned" by the people of India; therefore, in theory the Minister protects them in the public interest and in people's interest from external and internal dangers. Schools and colleges are regulated in the interest of poor people. So politicians at the time of Independence were close to gods in terms of "power" and therefore, the bureaucrats who serve the politicians became the next most powerful.

But with liberalisation and globalisation and the resultant removal of many controls in the economy and due to rationalisation of tax schemes to align with WTO (World Trade Organisation) regimes, the economic clout of politicians has been reduced during post-1991 (in India), and therefore, that of bureaucrats. The economic reforms brought in rich business persons in the limelight. They had much more freedom to invest without many Government controls. Since foreign direct investment (FDI) was also allowed to enter much more liberally (in fact sought after by politicians) and also due to much faster growth of economy due to reforms, various forms of illegal black money generated earlier under the centralised socialist monopolist economy started flowing into Indian economy (Few will admit it in public debates!). So, there are many more wealthy persons in India, competing for limelight. Many of them are far richer than many corrupt politicians. But still they cannot usurp the political power because many of the earlier public sector systems and Government controls are in place. There are many Government regulations to deal with. Also there are public sector purchase orders—be it for roads, health, education, irrigation, etc. These are controlled by politicians in power. Politicians can suddenly impose price controls or export ban even for a short period, under the pretext of public interest. While situation is lot better now than what it was in the 1970s or 1980s, still business persons are at the mercy of politicians who can "fix" them with some tax cases or hold back clearances for environment or land or similar such clearances. But still the imperial positions of the political power structure have diminished. This is mostly because the elections became very costly and many small parties have mastered the political game of identity politics. The party machinery consumes a lot of money as only a few party workers will work for ideal goals. Most of them use party machineries for their own good living and their own feeling of power at the local levels or state levels or national levels.

Therefore, politicians have to be dependent on wealthy persons of business, trade, bankers, etc.

Thus the heights of political power structure are not as high as it was before, in countries like India. In addition, multiple social groups are asserting themselves through smaller parties and regional parties. Thus the coalition politics brings down icons periodically and throw in newer ones.

But still political power is of highest level of hierarchy in India and will be so for many more years. In theory anybody can enter it. But in practice nowadays, after three generations of politicians, there are dynasties at all levels. These are entry barriers. However, if some emotional-local causes can be captured to get some critical number of seats, political power comes to that group. Emotional issues can be religion, caste, sub-caste, local poverty, water, unemployment, etc. It has to be "sensed" at the local levels. It need not be a noble cause. But it should capture the attention especially of the youthful voters (See also some other forms of powers in the hierarchy given in the subsequent sections. They can be used to climb up.). Of course it is difficult to do clean politics in India now. May be so in future too. But it will continue to be powerful at least for next few decades. Even though the dynasties are going to be stumbling blocks to rise up, if a political aspirant can muster locally a critical number of seats then his/her bargaining power with the dynasties goes up as a coalition partner.

Money Power

Close to political power in the hierarchical structure is the money power that is related to business, trade, agriculture, speculation, real estate, services, finance, etc. Any path that makes one rich is the path to power—money power. This is so in all developed countries as well, though most people may not stand in awe for them as they do in the developing countries.

In developing countries like India where poor are in majority and middle class is a small percentage, the small group of rich persons can almost do anything they want, especially if they can have a quiet alliance with the political system. Once you have money, it multiplies several fold especially in a fast growing economy like India even if one is not smart enough. Capital is a scarce commodity in India for most people; therefore, the rich rule. The ambitious (and often gullible) middle-class persons put their savings in the hands of these money-powered persons through stock exchanges, lotteries, new investment schemes, etc. They hope to get riches along with them and also suffer huge crashes (some of them artificially engineered too!).

While there are a number of honest business persons or traders who often find it difficult to survive in India without pleasing the ubiquitous corrupt systems and also use not legal methods due to the opaqueness of the governance systems and inordinate delays in the legal systems. Therefore, money power is not an unmixed blessing for the practitioners. They require various forms of political and bureaucratic patronage which can often be "bought" with right amount of money. Hence money power has considerable clout with those having political power. Price paid by electoral democracies is to make the politicians dependent on those with money power for funding elections. In countries like India this dependence is much more because the middle class is too small yet powerful and to woo the voters who are poor people, mostly Indian politicians have devised many novel techniques requiring large expenditure of money in elections and otherwise.

Those of you who want to acquire money power, need to learn many tricks of the trade, not all of them would be "clean" especially at the entry levels for the new comers. Starting a new business with small sums of money with sold family properties and becoming a millionaire, etc. will be mostly so rare that they would be mythologies spread by those who have become successful by using all sorts of methods earlier and with money power thus acquired, they can afford to preach others about ethics.

For entry from a relatively low income levels and then to rise higher is far more easier in countries like USA, Israel, etc. which have well developed venture capital systems. In the USA, in the earlier years of the twentieth century, some of the venture capitals had mafia connections! Now, of course, they are different—modern and professional. In fact success of persons like Bill Gates, Hewlett, Packard, and many others are equally attributable to the soundness of the USA's venture capital systems than merely to the "brains" of these individuals. In India many with ideas and brains struggle to get initial funds.

Those who can raise something like a few crores of rupees by mortaging their properties can, of course, go up if they use tricks. Those who have only a few thousands or a few lakhs of rupees will find it hard and get caught in "smallness" but if you keep looking, there are some intermediaries – not so clean – who help through the murky system. One has to be ready to do unethical practices like cheating in performances, accounts, taxes, etc. Also be ready for the mental pressures brought in by such "non-clean" methods. But to rise through the initial ladders of your search for money power these things help and perhaps are essential.

That brings us to the next hierarchy of power in the Indian context.

Crime Power

Crime power has gone high up in hierarchy of powers in the modern times (world over). Not that it did not exist earlier in many centuries. But those who indulge in it did not have a social standing. But with increasing globalisation and formal adoption of "democratic processes" there is a need for those who hold political power and money power to do things which are not exactly legal but they do not want to do them directly. The ancient feudal political power had absolute powers and were not fettered by the modern constitutional processes and ethics! Such items can range from tax evasion, black money generation and its protection, paying money as illegal gratification (corruption), creating problems for those who oppose (in case of political power) and to those who compete with you (in case of political power and money power-holders) and more virulent forms like threatening, attacking and even eliminating. Most of us talk about it; there are constant rumours; some news items; many coverages in modern literature, be it short stories or novels or even in poems; movies, TV serials, etc. There are some well-researched articles and books highlighting the dimensions of the problem.

It is not a phenomenon unique to India. In many developed countries there are organised crime networks. In the era of globalisation, the global capital needs them; these crime networks use the global capital networks. Banking systems in a number of countries are specially tuned to facilitate and transact money (including black money!). Even illegal transfer of huge amounts of money receives full protection of secrecy, because of the secrecy provisions in these countries. Secrecy of business transactions can also easily use these secret illegal networks. Also almost all defence procurements around the world are clouded in secrecy. In one sense, it is understandable because you don't announce to the world what equipment or arrangements you are buying, what training you are taking, etc. On the other hand, it is not one single manufacturer but many companies from many countries are competing for supplies. These are huge contracts! Politics increases the desire to maximise the purchase orders placed on companies in their countries because such orders increase employment figures in their countries; therefore people in their countries love such a situation of increase in job opportunities. Why should they care which weapons are sold to whom? Such a competitive seeking for defence orders (by purchasing and seller countries) shrouded in secrecy, breed many crime networks; in fact, they can sustain only with crime networks. That is the reason we periodically hear of new scams in arms deals, aircraft deals, etc. in the developed and developing countries.

In addition to these defence deals and other security related deals in India, we have encouraged our environment for corruption and crime networks right from 1960s through various Government enacted laws, controls and rules on social and economic lives, like prohibition, very high taxes on income, as much as 90 per cent of the total income!; prohibitively high customs duties on things like watches, electronic goods, almost any thing!; severe controls on foreign exchange, etc. In such a controlled regime our crime networks grew rapidly and developed international connections (As a young boy of 13 during 1957, I have directly seen how illegal liquors were sold in Bombay now Mumbai! At later period shaving blades, watches, etc. were smuggled through.).

The licence permit-quota-raj which throttled private sector enterprises developed a wonderful network of political-money (business)- crime network. How much of film industry in Bollywood was born out of crime network is well known! In nature, none of these can be of unidirectional flow. They mix, interact, sometimes integrate. Politicians learn to use black money to win elections; then engage in crime to retain political power; they also enter into business to have direct money power for themselves. In a later period, crime power-holders also became business persons and politicians.

Now we have a dangerous alliance of political-money-crime powers in India, much worse than in many developed countries. It is worse still because it is directly affecting the daily lives of many Indians (unlike the situation in developed world where these nexus do not directly affect people often on a daily basis). The fact that we are better than some of the developing countries in Africa, Central Asian countries or Latin American countries should not make us feel good.

There is another facet to the crime power. Humans don't live by bread alone. There are feelings, emotions; feelings of superiority, of insecurity, of alienation, etc. Also sometimes a firm belief that they alone are right, leads to extremist thinking in religion, in language, in a sect or in an ideology. People take to violence. You see it all over the world. These crime networks will continue with humanity for a long period. But they will be confined to small pockets if countries are better governed in the overall.

So far I have given some suggestions in earlier sections which those youths who desire power may like to try. But for crime power (though it is the third in the level in India), I pray that our youth do not get into. However, in pursuit of earlier said two powers they may have to 'brush shoulders' with some crime power. That is the reality of India now. I also appeal to the youths to find innovative ways to get into power without criminal links.

But crime power will never go above political and money power in any functioning country having democracy, dictatorship or any other forms of governance. The moment it reaches the top, the countries will collapse into major civil wars—as it is happening in some African countries now.

Media Power

Though media is described as the fourth estate of a democracy after the legislative, executive and judiciary, Indian media went through severe constraints even after Independence. TV, Radio, etc. were completely state controlled and were the puppets of the ruling party at the centre (Even State Governments could not control them, in the way they would have liked them.). Somehow even the judiciary in that period did not seriously question such a role of the Central Government.

Only in the print media there was greater freedom. But even then the control on import of newsprint (i.e. paper for printing), on printing machinery, etc. made media dependent on the state power, i.e. the administrators and politicians. Later Government advertisements were used to exert pressure on newspapers which publish news against the ruling government. During the period of emergency (1975-76), of course, there was direct danger of arrest, injury, etc.

Also since the Government completely controlled the economy during the licence-permit-quota raj period (i.e. till 1991), the administrators had great power. They were number two below politicians (I describe them as the power of the State in this write-up.). Executive, including judiciary and legislative all exercise the State power. Major chunk of it was with the executive which with various oppressive (colonial rule derived) rules kept Government officials under severe control of senior officers. Top administrators were virtually 'feared' by everybody—businessmen and media (like the *maharajah* under the British administrator of the past).

But to some extent technology exerted pressure on this oppressive situation. Availability of copying machines and fax machines during the 1980s (liberalised imports effected by the Central Government during 1977 and continued beyond) helped many journalists to venture into investigative journalism—copied sheets of Government files were 'smuggled through' by some daring persons. Availability of straight long distance (STD) calls allowed much easier spread of news from various parts of the country. Though some of these processes were helpful to 'liberate' press from the control of Government, even after the advent of satellite communication in India in the 1980s, TV and radio were still under the State control.

It is only during the last decade of the twentieth century, as a part of economic reforms, TV and radio got their 'freedom'. Many private enterprises including foreign ones started broadcasting in India. Cable TV networks facilitated many channels to reach the households at a cost affordable to them. Even many slums in the cities and rural areas started receiving many of these channels. Now literally, with explosion of channels, there are several news channels which offer information round-the-clock. Though sometimes they turn out to be a great nuisance (often depicting violence, rape, etc. sometimes even 'cooked up' news as it has happened in a few cases.) such a TV and radio coverage had also revolutionised the print media. Modern communication, computer and imaging technologies have further helped the print media to have speedy, fast and flexible coverage (even for customising to local needs to cover a group of districts – as a supplement or a few pages, etc. to the main 'national' newspaper). Thus the media power has truly born with this great freedom.

Media power in India has now gone to the fourth position after the trio of the hard powers described above. This is not so in many other developed countries. Due to the complex nature of our society and the middle class which has seen some wealth in the post-liberalisation period, the media power acquired a unique dimension. Since social space available is yet very small, there is a competition to appear in TV, to have photos in certain pages, etc. These give a large satisfaction to those who want to be powerful. Many are "known" through media. Also globally, human rights have acquired a new strength as also various forms of environmental activism. Many NGOs (Non-governmental Organisations) promoting these causes have become a major chunk of service industry. These changes have also influenced the attitude of the judiciary to things reported by the media. Hence media has become powerful. Also there are a few major players who are able to invest more money and organise their news delivery in an aggressive and catchy manner as is done in many advanced countries.

Business persons try to use the media to build up their image. It helps them a great deal when they go to a public issue to raise capital from small investors. Politicians and political parties work overtime to project themselves in a favourable image and to tarnish their opponents, (enemies?). Thus from a totally dependent and money-starved situation, Indian media has emerged as a wealthy industry, employing many persons with good income and also trying to exert their pressures on Government and businesses. So much so even those who are supposed to have systems which have rigorous internal discipline such as scientists, spiritual leaders, etc. have started using media to project themselves. If you appear in a news you are a "big scientist" whereas the peer group evaluation in science universally is not supposed to depend on this! So with spiritual *gurus*!

Unfortunately, one cannot say that media has emerged as a saviour to purge Indian society of its evils like corruption, hypocrisy and crime. The main reason is that media is also a business. It has to be profitable and be market driven. In an effort to win markets (not just the readers but most importantly advertisements) media bosses adopt many techniques which cannot be fully certified as ethical practices. To win advertisements and to get sponsors for events in TV, radio, and other mass media, various practices under severe competitive pressures are adopted. All types of practices are adopted to best the competitive pressure. Such practices or 'malpractices' to increase the viewers' ratings, to report increase in circulation for newspapers are not small in number. In addition, many good news on oneself (be it in print, TV, radio) and bad news on competitors, can be 'bought' for a price; such 'buying' can be at the highest levels of media to smallest levels of reporters, etc. The rise of PR (Public Relations or advertising) agencies to promote the brand of company, or institution or a political party or individuals, etc. is a clear indicator of existence of many such practices in the media. It is a big business which is intricately intertwined with the top three trio of power hierarchy and uses the bulk of the middle class and also semi literates as their "factory" to churn out their emotions to gain benefits. Such lobbying, PR, and (mis)use of media are prevalent in developed democratic countries as well. In fact Indian systems follow them in many ways. However, as explained earlier, since the social and economic space available to middle class is very small, such media actions acquire special power in India, much more than what it is in the developed democratic world.

In addition, individuals in pursuit of their own (selfish) ends—wealth, recognition, etc.—also distort ethics in media. Some of them are even known to resort to threats to vulnerable persons in business and politics to get their ends.

The growing acceptance of media power can also be seen in the fact that the recipients of Padma awards from media are increasing.

The rise of big money and new-found power equations have also brought media close to the crime power. Do they expose all the criminal links? Do they bring out all the truths? The answer sadly is 'No'!

Yes, media has become another active tool of power politics. Also a constant exposure in media can create many new celebrity figures. For youth in search of power, media power is definitely a good option. It brings in good income and also a quick access to corridors of power. But one has to be aware of the other interconnections. Also one should remember that watching and reporting as well as backroom gossips have their limitations. The trio of power is the real hard power now in India which have been explained earlier, i.e. political, money and crime power. The dependence of media power on the other three too will continue. Some media persons who push too much around with the other three persons may disappear as martyrs (often even un-mourned!). This is a caution one has to remember, especially in the Indian context.

State Power

By this I mean the power of the State as exercised through administrators, judiciary, police, etc. In a truly democratic country, under the ideal situation when the constitutional processes (in the legislative, executive and judiciary) work perfectly and in harmony (with minimum essential tension), the State Power should be the number one (Under administrators, I also refer to the ministers as decision/policy makers – not the "politicians" part of her/him but as the constitutional authority of the executive.). But as described under political power, (i) compulsions of elections, electoral funding, (ii) the complex sociology of parties (the Constitution refers only to the elected representatives and not to the parties and it is common knowledge that the political parties are the least transparent institutions in India!), (iii) the lure of black money which grew leaps and bounds in the post-Independence India and (iv) vast prevalence of feudal mentality among Indians – elite, middle class and the masses of people – etc., all of these contributing factors make the politicians detaching themselves from the ideal State and appearing as a separate power even when they occupy crucial constitutional positions. The letter of constitutional process and the complex web of the sociology of vested interests of the powers elevate the politicians to that level. In developed countries with mature democratic processes situation is different. The politicians are only nominally superior to those who exercise the State Power as regular administrators, etc.

But in India the gap is very high. As pointed out earlier, in the pre-liberalisation period (i.e. 1947-1991) the power instincts of the politicians coincided with the use of State power and it also gave them money power (mostly illegal!).

In the post-liberalisation period business persons acquired enormous money power. In addition, various mechanisms (as described earlier) allow the earlier 'dark energy' of black money to come out as grey and then white, a new creation of black money and the further cycles!

Thus the State power has fallen down not only in the ranking to 5th position but is well below that of the hard trio power and media. In the early years of Independence and even during the eighties, an IAS officer was a very powerful person. She/he could speak their minds. Presently most of them have been reduced to meek spectators of the power play of the hard power trio and media. Those who are so inclined also play the game and tend to rise up!

But in a constitutional democracy (and even more so in dictatorship) the State power will exist. Those who are in administration, police and judiciary, still will wield power, but will be overwhelmed by the other four. Of course, those who exercise State power can also use the overall corrupt situation (explained in earlier sections) to get their own benefits too (especially money power). A few martyrs within the system may be suppressed within the system and may feel happy that they are true to their conscience (I know a number of such persons too.).

For youth who desire such State power, there are several routes which they can take to through IAS, IFS, IPS, IRS examinations and examinations by the judiciary. Also if a whole set of youth join together, they may be able to fight the system (be careful please!) from within. Remember episodes like those of Manjunath. I wish such joint actions take place especially as a coalition of clean State power persons, clean Media persons also. It will be a great day for India if such groups of persons succeed and set new trends and clean up political, money power and greatly minimise crime power.

State power ought to be elevated to turn a true hard power, controlled by the constitutional processes externally and compassion of the power wielders internally (i.e. in their hearts). That will be the true spirit of Gandhiji's *Ram Rajya*. In fact it will also be ideal of a communist State which is in a withered state.

In the modern parlance, there will be democracies with deep humanism built in and global sustainability and inclusion as cardinal principles of actions.

Let us hope Indian youth can transform current India to such an India by 2030.

Mass Entertainment Power

Marx was not incorrect when he said religion is the opium of masses. Even though I have described about the *numero uno* position of political power, present number two position of money power, crime power and state power, the number of persons who exercise these power (or have these powers in true sense) is very small. In feudal times the kings, nobles, rich merchants, and many others were very small in number. In democracies their numbers may be much more than what was in the feudal period. Still it is a small percentage. For example, in India all those who are rich and powerful (political, money) would not exceed 100 million. Actual billionaires are only about 100,000. I have been more liberal in my above estimate to include those who with their political or money power can have small pockets of power and influence and feel good about it, though they may not even have a state level influence. If we use national level influence of power as yard stick, the number will only be about 10 to 15 million persons, in a country of 1 billion plus people!

Such a small percentage of power elite continues to rule despite the slogans of democracy. What about the developed countries? The number may be higher but never 50 per cent or even close to it. But the important difference between the developed countries with mature democracies and India is that in developed mature democracies the 'influence' wielded by the rich and powerful have little impact on day-to-day lives of common people. They do not drastically change the lives of intellectuals, those who oppose the establishment. The reason is that the social and economic spaces available to people in such developed and mature democratic countries is so large that the relative 'subjective' feeling of greatness of money or political power is limited; the space they cover in media discourses is relatively a small percentage if we take the totality of production of contents.

India is, of course, better than dictatorships and many other developing countries. But we have a long way to go. In India still, it is the powerful who 'rule' and determine the destinies of others – open and close the doors of narrow spaces of social, economic spaces and even in literary, artistic fields! Pure merit has little space; patronage of the powerful and privileged access to the powerful are vital even in ordinary people's lives. It is true even at the 'grass-roots levels' of democracy for ordinary and poor people – to get a ration card or identity card for 'below poverty line' or to get money from Government schemes or to get even casual jobs with local contractors or to get Government jobs or a job of teacher, etc. Even here the powerful people levy their 'dakshina' (holy fees) like a priest before the deity of power.

Thus we have a large number of people – poor persons, low and middle-class persons, educated persons, creative persons, etc. – who have very little power to lead their own lives in peace and to their liking, though the Constitution provides for equality. In reality there is little equality in India. How to keep these large masses of people under control? one needs an 'opium to be given', a simile or a metaphor, Marx used to describe how feudal societies with great inequalities maintained their, social peace through the use of religion.

In the modern times, other technological tools have entered: TVs, lotteries, quizzes, etc. To be sure the developed and mature democracies also use these mass entertainment techniques. Perhaps without these entertainment avenues, a large mass of people may not be able to play the games of their lives (read *The Games the People Play*, a classic by Eric

Berne). In India, we have other earlier perfected tools of religion, spiritual practices, mythologies, belief in magic formulae, social taboos, and so on.

Thus under the mass entertainment power, there are different factors which have prominent role to play in this field. They are:

(*i*) Spiritual-religious-leaders, yoga teachers, preachers and others; some of whom have resorted heavily to TV, radio and other print media. These leaders often have a huge network coupled with other three hard power trio (I don't say all of them are bad. However, it is difficult to assert that all are good. There is a large number of them who are in the 'thick' of power broking; power sharing; power enjoyment, etc.).

(*ii*) Media entertainment of various forms – serials, mythologies, new stories based on beliefs in magic, and other newer forms of western entertainment including exposure of women's bodies, gory violence in many scenes, many new heroes sporting violence, wisdom and omnipotence (superman or superwomen) being attributed to the celebrities, cartoons, and other. Also many advertisements, sports especially cricket or quiz shows, and other mass entertainment are a huge business.

(*iii*) In addition to the above, India has its own unique brand of mass entertainment through political rallies. It creates many myths around dynasties of leaders, new aspirants and new heroes. Those with money power and even criminal power can enter into political mainstream, through large size posters, public rallies and hired crowds to boost the image of mass appeal. Many youth in the country especially those who are school drop-outs, or unemployed after meagre education (not at all their fault) find a great thrill in such rallies and processions which often times become violent. All the same these rallies keep the huge mass of people engaged to make them feel that they are doing a great job. List of new opium is large.

(*iv*) Not to be left out there is a great resurgence of many earlier religious practices – in all religions. More pilgrimages, more of ritual fasts and (padayatra) walking distances on specific days. What used to be a private affairs of small groups have become major public events with powers-that-be trying to show their concern for the devotees and facilitating arrangements for others in their long holy trek (but making sure to publicise that so and so has done this facility). Ministers and Chief Ministers belonging to atheist parties also do this with religious groups of various types (often keeping an eye on electoral banks!). *Vaastu*, astrology (daily/weekly), lucky gems and others are emerging with all the wrappings of technologies.

(*v*) Other modern opiates are many. They also form hybrids with ancient Indian practices: new *yoga gurus*; organic foods almost promising immortality; success gurus; 'internal peace' *gurus*; fusion music; personal access to many pornographic materials; cyber world fantasies; games like cricket, and so on.

All of them compete to capture followers and viewers, because it is direct money or indirect money through advertisements, viewer ratings, and of course, benefits fame, feeling of celebrity, many much publicised awards; international travel, etc.

In simple economic terms, these whole set of activities is a major service industry. It forms a considerable chunk of the GDP (Gross Domestic Product) and creates many employment avenues. Above all, these activities keep down the individual frustrations under check, and give an apparent 'feeling of good' – the feel good factor. If one tries to pull out the large mass of the 'opiated' people to cultivate scientific temper or rationality, it does not seem to work unless science, or rationality itself is delivered as a mass opiate! We are aware of the mass movements in the south in the name of rationality and what has happened to them. Similarly, scientist-politicians (i.e. those who do power politics under the garb of science and try to acquire State power, money power and even political power) are using the appalling ignorance in our country especially amongst the elites as to what is really science; what does a scientist do; what does a technologist do; what is a science manager, etc. Scientist-politicians as one group of the actors under this mass group entertainment categories, distribute their forms of opium: India a great superpower; Indian brain is better than others; India's ancient knowledge makes Indians great scientists, etc. They spout many new words periodically like super conductors, nanotechnology, nobel prizes, 'catch them young', genetic revolution, confluence of IT, biotechnology, ever green revolution, climate change, etc. Also martyr version of Kalpana Chawla invokes deep feeling; hero worship of Sunita Williams adds to their glory!

I used to get agitated against all these versions of opium distributors, right from my youth days. I thought scientific, industrial and economic development of India will take care of weakening of these opiates.

But alas! I realise that I am wrong. I am understanding India's power structure much more clearly now, after working with several segments of Indian society over the last forty years since 1964. It is a strange hybrid of the older feudal systems (which are very strong), modern technological applications along with the external glittering of modern democratic constitutional processes. There is freedom of speech though all persons may not be heard, even in small meetings! Some who dare to disturb the existing power structures through talking or writing may be severely punished or suppressed.

In this strange milieu of past and present, discerning persons can daily see, many contradictions : stark ground realities and outwardly spoken hypocrisies; as well as great promises and little performance. But these contradictions will exist and be supported by higher power elites because there is a strong need to keep large sections of people in a state of 'feeling good', 'hoping for better', and so on. That is the reason why strong and diverse forms of 'opiums' are very important to keep Indian society 'peaceful'. Therefore the hard power trio will support this 'mass entertainment power' and they need them to be turmoil-free for their own powerful existence.

But this mass entertainment power is ever dependent on all the five power hierarchies mentioned above. Sometimes it may appear that they are celebrities – actors, spiritual or religious leaders, scientists and artists – but they are dependent on the superiors in the power hierarchy. As long as they serve the overall cause of the upper power elites, they will be safe in their profession and enjoy the shared power.

For many youth this route can be easier; they can gain popularity and celebrity status. But there are severe competitions. If you strike some innovative role model around you, you can successfully climb the ladder to this power. Of course, you have to be ready to put up with a hypocritic life you have to lead or with the masks which you have to wear and to change them often. There will also be slavery imposed on you, from the more powerful ones within this group. You should act as a slave but constantly try to raise yourselves.

Emotion Power

In most well developed countries with mature democracies, it may be difficult to create a special emotion power except when the society as a whole is threatened. The tragic event of 9/11 is a classic example in the recent times. In the post-war western world especially in USA, fear against communism was a great emotion that could be played upon during Cold War days. Then it was nuclear weapon proliferation for some period. Occasionally, there is the fear of spread of some diseases.

Often such emotions are to be generated by the executive of the government in such developed countries. Very rarely opposition to organised Government can create some emotion power. Some exceptions were seen during the time of Martin Luthur King; then anti-Vietnam war demonstrations, after a long period of opposition. European countries like France have more of emotional outbursts. There were youth agitations in Europe and USA during 1968.

But in developing countries with democratic set-up, invoking of emotion power is relatively a rare incident. It is sporadic and difficult to predict. That is the reason many developing countries often get into periods of suspension of freedoms or outright dictatorships. Sometime the dictators use the emotion power to legitimise themselves!

India has its freedoms of association and speech and a functional electoral system. But with the suffocating governance systems with administrative as well as judicial delays India is in a peculiar situation. Therefore the pent-up frustrations are huge and widespread. These are often stoked by political parties or others including crime power-holders to create disruptions. They can force a constitutionally and properly processed actions to be rescinded. That is, they can achieve their ends by using mob power, irrespective of whether they are right or not.

In the current phase of Indian history where no single party is able to dominate the centre and even the states, coalitions of various sorts are formed with fragile majority. In such a situation it is easy to have protest marches, *bandhs*, even violence, etc. to paralyse the Government in power from taking decisions. During the past decade or more, one notices a phenomenon where executive Government dilly-dallies on decision making—making the courts to intervene and decide. Then they can tell the opponents or agitators or partners that it is the Supreme Court that took the decision! If such a trend continues, then soon in the future, the agitators will train their emotions against Supreme Court and other courts.

The media power has joined with those who stoke emotion power often on the promise that they just report news. There are a number of occasions in which small isolated agitations or protests in some parts of the country are blown out of proportion and emotions spread like wild fire creating problems in many parts. One classic recent case is Gujjar agitation. There are many other cases which we frequently come across.

Unfortunately, India is passing through a phase where emotion power is stoked by somebody or another under some pretext or another – price of onion, religion, language, a particular tax, school admission, reservations, water sharing, etc. Some persons may feel that it is democracy in action; they may feel that it is a vibrant democracy. I am not so sure.

Every such emotional outburst puts back many decisions or projects aimed at development. When many countries in the world are capturing the economic and social opportunities available due to globalisation, India is still a slow mover. Those who suffer the most due to slow decision processes or actions or slow economic growth are not people who hold any of the powers listed above. They are ordinary people; they are poor people. Somebody agitates against a better yield giving agricultural practice; somebody against an industry... Also what is the sanctity of elections and the Governments installed after winning elections?

I do concede (as I have explicitly written in the earlier sections) that constitutionally elected Governments are not using the constitutional processes. Also for winning elections, the political parties are not using ethical and constitutional methods. I concede that money power and crime power are fully utilised in elections, at least before the Election Commission steps in with its processes. Party systems are opaque and there are feudal dynasties. It is also true that those who use money power often don't care about the welfare of people or environment and often use the corrupt political power..."So we need to fight against them" is the argument of the protestors and those who unleash emotion power to stop what they think is wrong. Often limits are crossed.

But such emotion power cannot be sustained too long. Outbursts fizzle out. There is a lot of suffering for those who agitate and also much more for ordinary people. Only on a few occasions the emotion power wins – often it is all a sad *tamasha*. The leaders who kindle emotion power have to shift somewhere else or to some new cause. But the fact is that emotion creators have their power position in the modern Indian milieu. Those who are in upper power structures have to depend on them or plead with them even for a brief period.

Is it good for Indian people? Well, in case, you want to be in 'power circles', especially for young persons the emotion power – generation and deployment – can be a practical avenue. But beware of the pitfalls; you may be arrested for short periods; sometimes even beaten up. Of course, such punishments 'increase' your power. If you can master media interface, you can be an effective user of emotion power to enhance your own power in the power hierarchy described in this write-up and also within those groups who use emotion power. Other lesser groups will also invite you to lend support! Maybe sometime you may shoot up to hold political power!

Backroom Power

That brings us to the last of the power in the power hierarchy. As I had pointed out a number of times in this write-up, these power hierarchies are not isolated watertight compartments. There are several complex interdependencies between them. Sometimes they mix up. But definitely there are many interactions between them on a daily or even hourly basis or monthly basis. For example, a politically-powered persons may need an urgent help of media power persons or crime power or even emotion power.

A criminally-powered person may need a mass entertainment power-holder to help him/her with better image or even a political connection. Permutations and combinations between these seven power hierarchies are many. There are many individuals and institutions which facilitate these interactions very rarely with glossy public events but often times totally behind camera, unknown to many persons. History may not capture them at all. They are well known within the power circles. They are "backroom boys or girls". In the USA, some of them surface in public as lobby-makers. In India it is a dirty word. So backroom persons roam around with different names or titles or are simply invisible to the public. But within their groups they wield special powers: rich and the powerful may often "beg them" to do something urgently. They are sought after. They also climb up the ladder and can reach a stage where they will deal with the most powerful persons only; they may even ignore the lesser persons after they reach such a stage. Some of them may also receive many accolades or awards after they reach such a position. Yes, there is a great career advancement within this backroom power.

They will be in demand as long as power hierarchies remain. They can feel the power but not wield it. They may have to often feel like parasites. Sometimes they may be ignored; they may have to gulp their pride, often.

In India in the coming years this backroom power may emerge as a major service industry and spread to linkages with global power hierarchies as well. That is because of rapid globalisation of Indian economy and society.

Youth can have lots of opportunities if they are beware of risks and pitfalls. If you are too ambitious in this role, you may lose out to your competitors. If you are too passive you may be used and thrown out as a waste paper. But those who want to enter into power circles, this can be an easy route. If you remain too long in it without trying to enter the upper power structures you may have to remain there eternally.

4

What is the Modern *Arthasastra*?

The ancient great work of Kautilya (around third century B.C.E.) was kept secret so that a few select practitioners from the feudal upper hierarchy can use it for becoming kings, winning wars, ruling their kingdoms, and above all keeping themselves safe from various forms of palace conspiracies and machinations of internal and external enemies. It elaborated about diplomacy and war.

In addition, it elaborated on how to raise finances from taxes and other means. How to use them.

It also specified how the king or an aspirant king has to regulate himself. That great work drew upon many experiences and existing knowledge bases. Then Kautilya or Chanakya used his theories to help make Chandra Gupta Maurya, the first great Emperor of India.

Many general principles about the nature of power, ambitions and frailties of human beings, are valid even now. But many other details of his great work are not valid. Modern day governance systems are different. Power has expanded to various other levels of society. Populations are large.

Communications are very fast. Women are also drawn into the society with equal measure.

In countries like India there is a huge churning taking place due to very fast economic growth as well as the processes of constitutional democracy, however, defective they may be in practice.

The globalisation and the resultant linkages have opened up new economic and social spaces for the satisfaction of "power-urges". The harsh punishment for the challenger to the power structures as it happened in the imperial feudal days are not exactly valid now, though at the entry levels at the lower echelons of the power structures (for example, murders in panchayati politics; or some violent shoot out in businesses like real estate at the local levels; or burning down of a media office or attacks on a editor or a reporter; ... to cite a few), such harsh realities exist even today in many parts of India, in different degrees of harshness.

As one rises up in hierarchy, the power games become more sophisticated. Violence as threat or punishment takes different forms. [For example, a politician in power may punish his administrator who is not pliant with vigilance cases; or another politician with CBI (Central Bureau of Investigation) enquiry; a person with money power may unleash negative campaign against a competitor or buy up his vendor chains, etc.].

With prosperity spreading to more people and with media images bombarding every segment of society, aspirations for power-wielding, the power urge goes up. Such aggressive and competitive behaviours are promoted by the society as important skills. Many youth face these realities today.

Therefore they have to learn about the realities of power structure. Remember those in power will never tell you how they really got there and how they are holding on. Those will be the real secrets as Kautilya taught the young Chandra Gupta.

Yes, if they tell the truth, their positions may be endangered. They may cease to be celebrities or supermen or superwomen. They will give speeches or write articles and books about merits of hardwork and steadfast adherence to truth and ethics. They will create new myths and visions for the young; new opiums for them. Because they have to be safe. This applies to all the eight levels of power hierarchies, including the scientist-politicians, knowledge-politicians and spiritual-guru-politicians as we discussed earlier.

This work is an attempt at the contours of modern Indian *Arthasastra* (twenty-first century first half version – it may change later!). It tries to lay bare the real ground realities. For obvious reasons names of actual persons are not mentioned. You can imagine about many persons who will fit in many of the characteristics or attitudes described here. Try to do such fits to sharpen your understanding of the dynamics of power politics (This is to be done secretly. Don't blabber about it even after a few drinks!). You may be wrong in some cases. You will learn as you observe, think and as you later practice.

How to take first steps? Not easy. But you have to take a plunge. You may be bruised. Keep your tenacity. But no fixed goal or path, please. You have to be alert, agile and flexible to change paths and targets. Look at how politicians change; how business persons change their strategies; celebrities change the field of actions; editors change their ideas or allegiance. Your goal should be your success and everything that will lead to it. Yes, it is an amoral and utilitarian world.

You may have to wear many garbs and many masks. You should not be shy of it or ashamed of it.

You may ask me what about the value system you have inherited or your conscience. Well, it is yours. Either you have to learn to tame them or be tamed by them! If you are tamed, you may not reach the top of the power structures! Maybe sometimes those at the top may viciously throw you out!

Does it sound fearful? Well, power game is not for those who are "chicken-hearted". If you want to quit, you can become a follower or enjoyer of one of those mass entertainment power-holders and complete your cycle of life on the earth! Or be doing your routinised work and live like a worker bee or ant.

Life offers many opportunities. This modern work of revisited *Arthasastra* is for the current-day youth who feel the pangs of power-urge, who want to become powerful. For whom not being powerful gives sorrow.

Beyond all these power-plays, there are two categories called knowledge power, and moral power. They do not form the power hierarchy of the current day world. They are outside it. To a certain extent knowledge power can be put at number nine as it has some role in the developed world. Due to globalisation even persons from developing world can acquire it and have some role abroad. Hence, under Section-II, in Tables I have included it.

For all others who have a high PQ which creates in them an urge to pursue power, this book gives considerable clue to prepare themselves for the journey to power. While you have to learn from real life, visit the pages of this book often to understand what is really happening and to make your own theory.

Knowledge Power

It can be in science, economics and sociology, and insights born out of experience and special skills. It can be in creative fields like arts, music, painting and dancing. No doubt, modern societies require them. In well-developed countries with developed democracies persons with knowledge power can have freedom of choice, not interfered by power structures, and have their own satisfaction through their work and its appreciation by peer group in their areas. Also they get paid reasonably well for their work. Some of them can also directly trade knowledge for huge sums of money.

But in India those with knowledge power are mostly in Government or Government-funded institutions where political power and state power (administrators in ministries) rule. Since opportunities are limited, knowledge works (which in fact they are), but are afraid of taking risks of losing jobs. They are, therefore, subservient. Some knowledge workers get the patronage of politicians or administrators and act on their behalf mainly to satisfy their own needs for power. Since knowledge is neither big business nor vote catching, politicians do not bother about it except for lip service. Administrators would not like to see knowledge workers assert themselves as they will lose their hierarchies (they have already gone down as I have described). Therefore, scientist-politicians or knowledge-worker-politicians are the gainers. They use the word 'knowledge power' but power of real knowledge never surfaces nor is sought for. It just remains with the scientist-politicians/knowledge-politicians level.

Such a situation is likely to continue in India for about a decade or more until those who hold money power (i.e. business persons and rich agriculturists) really need knowledge workers from India to survive in a competitive global economy. In today's India, they (i.e. those with money power) are surviving on the follower type knowledge imported from abroad – it can sustain due to low costs of Indian workers and economy of poverty. Till that time when it becomes necessary for the survival of Indian businesses to create their own knowledge base (and not limit to purchases from abroad), possession of knowledge alone will not give any feeling of power to the possessor. Either they should be satisfied with their own real knowledge acknowledged by discerning peer group or they have to enter into one of the eight real power structures as scientist-politician, knowledge-politician, etc. There are already a few persons operating in India in such political mode but not through real knowledge.

But I would recommend to those youths who do not care for such power hierarchies to acquire knowledge, go abroad for some time at least, learn new methods and keep themselves fit for the creation of world level knowledge and its utilisation. It is tough; sometimes can be very frustrating, when you see persons with much lesser capabilities thriving in India, because they have won over the scientist or knowledge politics! Again I know of scientists, artists, writers, and many scholarly persons who command vast resources of knowledge in themselves and create world class knowledge in India. They live quietly in India undisturbed by external politics. But they are endangered species!

Moral Power

Under this, one can include good ethical behaviours, excellent value systems, clear conscience, compassion towards other humans and nature as a whole and respect for others. There are legends in India that those who possessed these qualities in abundance were respected and revered. Are they now existing? Perhaps there may be a hundred odd persons. But who notices them? Do not confuse these with persons holding mass entertaining power as they also preach values, moralities, suppression of ego and selflessness. I consider only those who truly practice them in their own lives' as those who have moral power. In the current phase of India, it is extremely unlikely that those who occupy any of the power hierarchies can have even a small amount of moral power (they may have knowledge!) as moral power is a scare commodity. I have been fortunate to know a few persons who had this power; also some who still have this!

5

Epilogue to the First Section

Thus on the whole, a combination of knowledge power and moral power will make great human beings. There may not be many in India now. Existence of even a few such persons will save the country or a society by their very presence even though they may not be known in the public domain.

I believe that India will grow economically despite its limitations. When it does so in two decades or less, spaces for social and economic opportunities will open up tremendously. Some idealistic persons may give up the rest of powers to integrate inside them knowledge and moral power. Many of our legends, mythologies, epics, heritage writings and folk songs emphasise these combinations. So many youths in future may discover these power (knowledge + moral) and imbue them in themselves and others. Their population will cross beyond a minimum critical size to make a difference for Indians, India, and the people of the world and world.

Well, till that time the eight power hierarchies will be dominant in India (and other parts of the world with different orders) may be with some alterations in their relative positions. What you want to do, you choose—understanding the ground reality and keeping in mind the clues and insights given in this small book.

Good luck!

Note : After a full understanding of the Section-I, go over to Section-II which will assist you in determining which facet of power quotient is better suited for you.

SECTION – II

Know thyself.

–Socrates

Power is the ultimate aphrodisiac.

–Henry Kissinger

Assessing Your Power Quotient

This section of the book puts together a set of check points to help you evaluate your own PQ. Before starting this section, it is important to read Section–I carefully, and internalise the insights contained therein before attempting to enter into this section. Also this section is not for one-shot marking. You may have to read it often when you are engaged in the long marathon of power. It can also help in the later years to reorient yourself or to do mid-course corrections. It has to be your secret companion!

6

Practical Considerations for Entering Power Structures

In the earlier section, we have dealt with the theoretical considerations regarding the complexities of the various facets of power quotient. The Section-1 addresses real life considerations and ground realities, especially in the Indian context. It is important to understand them very well. If you are interested in political power, do not confine yourself only to that. Those who can understand the intricacies of various facets of power quotient really win the game of power. It also helps to survive in a world of ruthless competition through tactical withdrawal to other areas and also to increase their power quotient. A front line politically-powered person may at difficult times get into media power or even backroom power and emerge at the right time to conquer the front position political power.

Think in your mind about such personalities. They are great survivors. Only survivors win the power games.

In good old times, leaders, kings, religious leaders, preachers, military leaders, and others used to run away from kingdoms where they had problems. They survived somewhere else and emerged back into the kingdom from which they had themselves ran away. Some became emperors, great religious leaders, and rose to some eminent position after such re-entry. Indian, European, Arab or any country's history is full of such examples (To be sure, there are also cases where people get ex-communicated and die as exiles! But as I have repeatedly stated in Section-I, those who want to climb up the power hierarchies have to be ready to take risks, sometimes even risk their lives! But modern constitutional democratic societies offer enough avenues to survive. You may not climb up the ladder. But your life may not be in danger. Also with globalisation being a day-to-day matter now, you may even decide to shift your life to another country and live a reasonably good life there. Thus there are many advantages to the modern power gamer. In the ultimate, you need not to starve to death!).

So, it is essential to have a good conceptual understanding of different facets of power quotients and their interconnections. Therefore, it is important to read Section-I carefully. I have kept it small knowing the time pressures of modern life. Also try to review Section-I once a year. You will get new insights, which are your own and, therefore, much more valuable.

In this Section-II, I have given certain checklists for assisting you to decide the paths you have to take, either at entry level or to change levels or to make mid-course corrections so as to help you explore the areas of activity as per your power quotient. The writing may be as observations and often as questions. No answers are given to the questions because you are dealing with your own life and lives of others. Be truthful to yourself and answer to them. You need not tell anybody as to how you answered them. In fact, you should not tell them.

Remember what was not done to *Arthasastra* of 3rd century B.C. It was not published as a general book available to public nor was it recited in schools. It was a closely-guarded document used only by persons who aspired for power – princes, kings, military strategists, and high-ranking personalities. In the modern day world, it is difficult to do so, as many more persons aspire for power and also population is far higher than it was in 3rd century B.C.

This book is divided into two sections. The first section provides an understanding and insights into the power aspirations among different groups of Indian youth and various facets of power quotient while the second section helps you evaluate your own overall power quotient. It also contains tables which will help you assess your power quotient and take right decision to move further the path of power.

The table has five point evaluations for facets of the power quotient. Your own reading of the eight (plus one) sub-sections of the power quotient as given in this section, the answers that come up in your mind, the insights you accumulate, etc., will help you to fill up the table—the only exercise given in this book.

The evaluation of the markings in the table will assist you decide as to how you rate yourself for different facets of power quotient and your power quotient if you mark them truthfully (i.e. as you feel it is with you and not as what you think it should be. Remember, it is not a test. It is your life decision.).

What is marked once, does not have to be so till your life's end. It is for a beginning or beginning for a change, if you are already in the game. But since life is evolving, your change and other's change, once in six months you can revisit the contents of this Section-II (preferably all the eight plus to sub-sections and the table) and re-evaluate yourself. It will help to stay on course or make mid-course corrections.

True to the style of the modern world, this modern *Arthasastra* is in your hands. It is for you to shape your future and enhance your power quotient.

Now let us get into the intricacies of power quotient. Have a calm mind and relaxed attitude when you read these sub-sections and do the exercise in the table (For actual actions, however, you often have to be passionate and energetic!).

Sub-Section-1

Political Power

1. How deep and how strong is your desire to have power over others, to be respected by others and/or to be feared by others?

2. How much you are ready to sacrifice your personal pleasures to achieve that goal?

3. Are you willing to part ways with your near and dear ones and friends, to fulfil your desires to be on the top?

4. Have you got any idea as to what is your entry level? Is it local? Or covering large area of the State? Or national level?

5. If it is at the national level, do you have some 'god fathers or 'god mother' to whom you can attach yourself? Will it lead to mere slavery? Or are you confident of working your way up?

6. Similar questions for the State and local levels. What are your genuine answers?

7. Do you have some 'unique selling propositions' (USP) which can get you affiliation of voters? For example, belonging to a particular dominant caste, or religion or linguistic group? Or can you capture the imagination of people by involving some emotional issues? Or a great ability in oratory?

8. Do you have a possible entry into a closed groups of some powerful political dynasties?

9. It is difficult to enter into the Indian politics without affiliation to a party. Do you have any party in mind?

10. If you are already a powerful attorney, or business-person or a media person, that is, if you can bring some of your special skills into the party or to its leaders, for raising funds; for building up public image; or assembling crowds for the visit of 'bigwigs' or writing powerful speeches, for them, or getting projects 'passed through' administrative approvals so that the bigger politicians can claim credit for themselves, you may be able to enter into politics (Please note that actually you are entering as a back room power. Does not matter. But you should look for yourself to come of your own even in a small territory or climb up to support higher levels of politicians.). Think of many such big party leaders, ministers, etc. who never had any grassroot experience, but are very powerful now. They followed this route. You will not find it in their biography or autobiography.).

11. If you have plenty of money (white or black)which you can spare for funding parties or select group of politicians for contesting elections, it is a good path. But you should know which parties/persons to

choose. People may cheat you. Are you clever enough? There may be other funders. If there are bigger or more powerful fund providers than you, then you will be sidelined even after they take your money! You have to answer these questions to yourself satisfactorily before you enter in this route. Another question, important one; if you have money to spare why struggle to be a politician, why not seek money power more vigorously and acquire more money, more money power (You can fund some media to project you as a great business person. You can make others to write articles about your achievements, abilities and good qualities, by rewarding them suitably, in a quiet and unknown manner. Similarly, there may be willing ghost writers who will give you excellent articles on payment. Your name can go up.). Yes, when you have money, there are other options. Therefore, you have to really search your heart whether you are ready to take all those risks (of abandoning all other easier possibilities) and chart unknown territory of politics.

12. If you are a woman and have capabilities for pursuing political activities (look at items from (1) to (10) above – and also have a strong desire to have dominating power over others, you have some unique advantages. All parties are looking for some women representatives. The gender issues (in a humanistic sense) may not be really in the hearts of hard core politicians, be they men or women, who are controlling party apparatus. But nowadays it has become a plus point to project themselves as gender conscious. So they would allow women to rise up to at least middle-level more easily.

    (It is not going to be a cake walk. But lot easier than equivalent level men. So you can try. Also are you confident to tackle the 'funny' behaviour of men in the system? What they look externally or what they speak for outside consumption, are not indicators of how men (or women) behave. So you should ask seriously whether you are bold enough to face a predominantly male world, which is cunning, ruthless, and feelingless. If so, you have an opportunity better than your equivalent men folk).

13. There are other methods possible too (for both men and women). Look at the power hierarchies carefully. You can be in the State power – be an IAS officer, State Government administrator or Income Tax/Revenue Service Officer, a Science Administrator or Public Sector Unit top brass. All that you have to do is to develop 'friendship' with a few political 'bigwigs' – local, state or national level. You should help them to project themselves (not you!!). You should help them in taxes (i.e. evasion and reduction) or get an approval for the politician's business activities or get Government purchase orders for their or their friends' companies. Then slowly become visible. Keep pushing up your image. Some day you can end up as a Member of Parliament or MLA or even as Minister. There are many examples during the past two decades.

14. The crucial thing is proximity to a politician (or a political group). You should know when to hang on and when to 'ditch'. That is a part of the political game. No long-term loyalty!!

Think about all these above items and other ground realities as they pertain to your ambitions. You will get good answers to the table and then in actual life. It will help you learn about your PQ.

Sub-Section-2

Money Power

1. Most people and particularly young are very keen to have lots of money. Young people are more open about it. But often it is for living a better life – a big bungalow or a posh flat in a metropolis, big car, lots of servants, fashion dresses, so much of enjoyment, and so on. All these are fine. These are all for consumption of money. Do you have ambitions beyond these to be the generator and owner of lots of money? Do you have an urge to be rich, mega rich? To create a money empire and get highlighted as a part of global rich, national rich and local rich? At the local level, your exhibition of richness can be in diamonds, gold, cars and "rich" looking dresses. As you aspire to rise higher, the exhibition of "richness" is much more subtle. Still they have a desire to be further rich. Do you have that burning desire?

   If yes, you are ready for money power. You can get it. Use it for enjoyment and also importantly to use that power to control others' powers!!

2. If you already have some base of money from your parents through land, properties and business, then

you have a good starting point. Don't always jump into the bandwagon business of that day. Yes, maybe one or two bandwagon type is ok. Your real success of having lots of money and money power can come only in the beyond the horizon business. It does not mean high tech. See those world scale company founders who invested on just simple retail like WalMart or in India in real estate when others were talking about automobiles and IT. In other words, you should be able to think beyond the usual something which is likely to emerge and risk your energies and resources. Of course, it will require a business plan and actions. You need to deal with politicians, bureaucrats, bankers, and others to enable faster movements. Maybe some "underworld" type persons. Do you like to do these things? Do you have the patience and tenacity?

3. In Indian situation doing business is lot more "free" than it was during pre-1991 when Government licence-permits, were the only requirements. Of course, for those who were politically connected and those who could "bribe" their way up, it was much easier. Then it was the question of "maintaining" your position by denying licence to your competitors. Post-liberalisation, this route alone will not suffice. To be sure, there are still dozens of crucial approvals where political patronage is important and essential (hence appropriate "bribing", etc.). Also unlike in the past, there is no single party system in the Centre or State. Coalitions and that too shifting coalitions are the order of the day. As one business person explained to me "*Jeb Ek Haath Anek*, i.e. the pocket (of money) is one; but (receiving) hands are many!" You should learn how to use your "bribes" wisely with short term and long term in view.

4. But current day business is more difficult because it is not just manipulation of politicians and bureaucrats. There are genuine business competitions from others. There are those who are better planned; there are those who have good and strong foreign parties. Also it is necessary to develop relations (some straight and some not-so-straight) with financiers. Also with media bosses so that when you go to public for raising capital, you are presented in better light.

   Even with all these complexities, doing business in India is lot more lucrative as the economy is growing fast. But you need a money base.

   Do you think you are understanding at least some of these elements?

5. Are you ready to travel? In the beginning years especially, are you ready to work 24x7? Though you have lots of money to deal with and even go to a five star hotel for eating, it is often difficult to be enjoying with your near and dear ones.

   Some investor may wake you up at night! Or you have to hang around in many parties just to develop networks. Or sustain networks.

6. It is difficult in India to do business in a totally honest way. Though "integrity" and "ethics" are talked about very often in public forums, profits are often maximised by not-so-honest ways. Purchase orders from Government contracts are obtained through privileged access which often may entail illegal gratification. So also from other illegal means mentioned before, this is real! The extent may vary. Are you comfortable with these? Some items may leak

out. There will be some additional tensions. Are you ready to take them in your stride?

7. On the positive side, to become a successful and powerful business person, you should be able to continuously assess the opportunities emerging in the horizon; learn from your global connections; business analysis reports. Are you willing to take pains to create a vision for your company and share it with others? Are you capable of exciting others, your board members, financial investors, employees, and others.

8. Though a few quiet, recluse business persons have been greatly successful, I think the 21st century will demand a large amount of communication skills to be a successful business person and to expand your empire. Are you having such skills and also ready to learn where you lack?

9. Are you capable of adapting to multicultural environment as business involves many global partners?

10. Are you capable of non-emotional decision making when you have to sell your existing assets in order to create a new opportunity?

11. Are you a risk-taker? Well, think about this world of entrepreneurship and business. It creates wealth for company, nation and the employees. Also a lot for you. But it has several features that will place heavy tensions on your mind. If you think you really feel for money power, take a plunge, after of course, duly evaluating yourself through the table in this section.

Sub-Section-3

Crime Power

This is a dark area in any society. Though there are many novels, movies and even biographies of great criminals or criminal groups of our times, how it all begins is often obfuscated. It will be more like a mythology. Not that the origins of political power or money power people are described with accuracy or with truth. Many murky beginnings are carefully left out (They will be available only as gossips!). But they rise up and flourish!

In case of crime power, such a closer observation is very difficult. When you had seen, he/she would have been an ordinary person. Years later you hear or see about him/her in print. Then you cannot see them!

I have no experience or contacts with such persons. Though I have to identify the actual existence of such persons in a book of this sort, which deals with ground realities, I would really like that our youth or others do not take to this route.

However, I have to raise a few points for completion, as there may be some persons who may be pushed to this area of power scheme, in their search for power.

1. Are you mentally prepared for this? Do you think of this route because you have no better option or do you get a "kick" out of it?

2. Do you realise that bulk of your life, you have to spend in the underworld?

3. Though the powerful ones, who induct you, will protect you from arrest or police. Do you realise that chances of your getting into the jaws of police or law are high?

4. Do you also realise that in the area of crime power there is constant danger of jealousy and betrayal within your gang and also from outside rival gangs?

5. And also, above all, once you get in any gang of crime power, it is difficult to get out? Even in a jail you will be chased by gangs?

6. Are you ready to be killed or decapitated and spend rest of your life, that way, if you can be lucky to survive?

7. The concept of family life may be completely shaken up and are you ready for it?

8. In a vast country like ours, there are many entry points from relatively simple items like arranging for bribery to carrying illegal substances or items or get into various forms of cheating, be it a land deal or purchases or chit funds, etc.

9. More sophisticated cyber crimes are reported in press. As a technical person, I can understand the modus operandi. But to do it in real life means lots of risks; you can be tracked and caught and punished!

There are many entry points. But don't think that you can enter for some period and get out later after you get some money. If money is the motivation, try other methods. If you get into crime power networks, it is very difficult to get out. But if you are confident and get a "kick" out of it, then that is a route to power.

Sub-Section-4

Media Power

Please remember media is not a glitter and glamour as it looks from outside. I know lots of people who are at various levels in media – print, TV and multi-media. Professional demands on a person's life are very high. You have to learn to forget the hours of work. Also about regular timings in day and night. You are on demand. Also you need to be looking out for news—to look for excitement. To create news!! Rush to a place, when you are about to take a late breakfast, where a VVIP is making an "inspired" speech. You have to fight your way through police cordon. Your press accreditation card is seen ten times at different places. If you don't have, you will be pushed out.

You meet many cynics, intellectuals, cheats and brags. Daily gossips release some tensions. But your health regimes take many "sixers", as you cannot eat properly. You have to sleep at odd times. More daring ones can go to dangerous zones of violence and warfare. You can also get some fame, if you are not killed or mutilated!

If you don't have god father or god mother or if you do not come from powerful dynasties, you have to start as a simple reporter. Run around. Have to change jobs to earn more and to find your way up.

Nowadays the best media power, is not necessarily with the best performers. It is the financial investors (many of them foreign ones) who hold the real power. They dictate often what policies to adopt. Whom to support? Whom to "witch hunt", all in name of truth, justice and fearlessness! You have to adjust the realities of media pressures and learn to change views (in writing) very often. Some questions you can ask to yourself are:

1. How passionate you are about writing? Often it is told that pen is mightier than the sword: but on whom or for whom you feel like wielding and using a sword?

2. Is it because you have deep hatred for some groups of people, or against some ideas (e.g. corruption etc.)?

3. Or do you have some great love for informing everybody about your special ideas?

4. Or is it just fun of meeting so many people? Travelling to different places?

5. Or is it to see your name printed everyday or week in papers, magazines and journals or appearing in TV as a reporter or anchor?

6. How strong you are in one or more languages? In writing?

7. Are you ready to spend your whole life as a reporter or a senior reporter and analyst, or do you have ambitions to become editor or chief editor? Chances of the latter are slim while as the former, you may have to be low in the hierarchy.

8. Are you aligned to any political party or ideology?

9. Are you ready to work at odd hours, eat at odd hours and sleep at odd hours? There are some who like this situation as it gives them a feeling of continued importance.

10. If your motivation is just getting a job and a reasonably good pay without too much of responsibility of delivery, then also media can be a good options–but this is not a profile of a person who seeks power. This book is about those who want to be powerful. Almost in all areas (even in political, or money making), if your targets are low, if you want more safety, it is different. Then you can take any profession and work well. Nowadays most professions, including media, give a good income, and reasonable stability if you are not too much ambitious.

11. If you are very ambitious and want to do something great in media, you have to take several risks. It is mostly power play, as you rise higher. Even when you are at a lower level you have to learn the tricks of power plays and align yourself with right persons with whom you can go up. Often change alignments. See, how many "star" anchors or reporters from one TV channel – who looked inseparable – just leave and join rival channels. You should be alert and be ready for it.

12. If you are in regions, say North East, or West Bengal or Tamil Nadu there is a possibility to rise up in the region. But big money and big advertising (be it for print or electronic media) are only around Mumbai and Delhi. Mumbai is primarily with money power and Delhi is both money and political power. That is why those media persons who are in Delhi and can position themselves well, get much more exposure

(be they chief editor or a TV reporter or a newspaper columnist).

13. Again as in politics you may decide to be a regional player and enjoy local/regional power/prestige. In such a case you concentrate on a region, its issues, dramas and also actively engage in power plays.

14. Another way can be to concentrate on some dramatic issues: protest movements; terrorism, crimes; climate change; health fads. Some items which capture public attention – make you something special.

15. There are people in media who specialise in celebrity-bashing, institution/industries bashing, and blackmail through these methods. Sometimes they work for their opponents who pay and also help you "rise up"; well, it is for you to decide. You can rise by a fast route but very risky too!

16. Nowadays since many foreign media are there, you can capture some international specialists and later enter India through connections (Or just enjoy international arena. Maybe your climb to power ladder can be more difficult, as those who are there already may place glass ceilings for you if you are the first time immigrant.).

17. Another tool of media which is emerging as a powerful one is in the cyber world: internet websites; blogs, and other networking sites. There are whole sets of new eyes and "mind" catches there. You could capture many of them. If you master new technology tools like animation, open source, search engine, and others. You have an added advantage in addition to writing. For example, if you can master the latest

trends of key words, you can ensure that you come up always in the search strategy. (This is like the media viewers' rating for TV shows.).

On the whole, media is growing as a large part of the economies of the world over including in those parts of the world where there is no great emphasis on "freedom of speech". Human beings need to talk, gossip, and get opiated with some entertainment. Hence media has a great role. However, whether you personally wield power, or feel powerful even in limited regions (if not at national level) it depends on several factors, we have given before.

You may turn out to be a "foot soldier" or a "worker bee" (This is true of other power layers too – political, money and crime!).

So read the above carefully and start making up your mind till you come to the last evaluating table.

Sub-Section-5

State Power

All constitutionally mandated or derived positions come under this category. Naturally, those who are Government servants – police, judiciary, tax collectors, inspectors from various wings of Government – those who give approvals (e.g. environmental clearances, land transfers, house plans) even those who are in Government hospitals serving Government servants, railways, educational administrations, S&T administrations, and others are parts of state power.

In the early period of post-Independence India, Government jobs were the most powerful and influential almost as close to those of politicians in power. It was partly because we inherited the British empire over India with very little change in power structure. Mostly British were replaced by Indians. Naturally many Indians aspired for such power which was obtained through IAS, IFS, IPS, etc.

Later the bureaucracy started concentrating power especially through the socialist pattern of development by nationalisation of banks; control of industries and private enterprise through licence-permit-quotas; control of educational sector; huge levy of taxes on individuals, corporate, etc.

It was more or less a "dictatorship" practiced through bureaucracy! Hence the State power was very high. Engineers, doctors, professors, scientists, and other high ranking persons came under the power of departments and ministries. Even the lowermost staff in ministries, deptt., Government offices were very powerful. The public (people) were to be mere subjects.

Within the bureaucracy there was a great network to favour itself. Even the judiciary depended for many things including the Government house allocation on bureaucracy. Journalists were given special houses in Delhi! Similarly, police had remarkable powers, though in theory the Constitution provided many power to the citizens. But these extraordinary powers also led to corruption and the formation of a crime network.

During the Emergency, empowered by the politicians, the bureaucracy exercised the highest of the State power. But later it also led to its downfall. Many in the bureaucracy were prosecuted or penalised. Later the weakened bureaucracy came under the control of politicians and also the crime networks. The corruption to which bureaucracy succumbed (partly for itself and partly for the political bosses), made it "subservient" to the power of those who have money and can give money to them and to the political bosses. During the 70s particularly since 1980s, corruption was accepted to be a national phenomenon openly!! That also brought down the power of bureaucracy, which really was (is) the State power! Even criminals can dictate terms to them! But, of course, for normal law abiding citizen, they can continue to be the terror.

During the post-1991 era, due to liberalisation, the bureaucratic, legal, etc. control on industry loosened. State governments got more power. Politicians became adept in bending the State power (thanks to the training given by the pliable administration and judiciary over four decades of rule).

Therefore, money power rose to second level while crime to the third level. Also since technology and liberalisation of economy brought many faster methods of communications, audio-visual devices, imaging devices and other such devices (including miniature electronic cameras), the power of the media has gone up. In countries like India where there is Western type democracy, media has followed some of the methodologies used in USA, UK, etc. to capture the minds of viewers and to keep the political system under great "tension". In the process media persons have also acquired power and they are not mere spectators and reporters. They also play active "power politics". In addition, the Right to Information (RTI) is not only a fashion but also it has been given legal teeth.

Therefore, the State power as exercised by those who have to be the real guardians of the constitutional processes have come down to the fifth rank.

But still the State power is important. May not give as much prestige, as it was in past.

But if you have a desire to be controlling the powerful, though for a short while (i.e. politicians, moneyed man, crime power man and media), State power is still important. Finally, every society operates through some governance mechanism, i.e. State power.

If you do not have any difficult feelings of being corrupt, the State power continues to provide many avenues, regularly all through the career.

Even at the bottom level of approvals, you have ability to exercise power. No doubt, you may get overruled or hit on head, some time or ordered around by a boss. But still you have many opportunities as the boss cannot be all the time supervising you!!

Even at the highest levels of Government, when political and money power put lots of pressure on you, by clever manipulation of media power, you can have your way – because the State power has to be exercised by the occupant of the Chair.

But those who hold State power cannot be in the limelight. Everybody knows that you are the Secretary to Government, Joint Secretary or DG, Police or Judge, but you cannot brag in public as politicians do; though money power persons do. You are supposed to act quietly!! If this does not bother you, you can aim for this.

If you are clever enough you can get into money circles too, after you rise up in State power levels as many top bureaucrats do.

Bulk of the State powers comes through organised services like IAS, IPS, IRS, legal services, etc.

You have to enter early by competing in the competitive examinations. There are many reservations based on castes and other considerations. Try to grab the opportunities.

Again going up is not through honesty, integrity or rules. Often it is the contrary. But you should learn it. With RTI in action you should be careful. If you are clever you will learn the "tricks of the trade" to earn extra and also to go up in life.

For academics, scientists and others who are not much in approval/inspector circles, opportunities are limited. But they have their own network (academies and institutions) through which the power games are played. Make it a point to get in there. Then catch the scientocrats who have access to State and Political power, learn to rise up. Often there will be "bloody" fights and betrayals. If you are in power game, you should learn to master it.

But by and large the State power comes through competitive examinations for organised services, examinations for judges, and many such examinations.

- Do it well!

- Do you have the capacity to keep waiting in your early career, say 10 years, to be subservient to come up?

- When you find many hypocritical statements are being made about schemes, can you just ignore them and be a part of the hypocritic games?

- Can you at least keep quiet and not block, when fraud on public is taking place before you?

- If you leave in a huff, even monetary benefits will go away. Chances in the outside world are low for an ex-bureaucrat (even an Engineer-turned bureaucrat) unless you have risen very high in Government. Even then business houses don't like to have "straightforward" persons. You should be "flexible".

- Can you do the above? Then prepare yourself for the competitive exams and capturing State power even at a State Government level! Avenues are limited. So do very well to qualify State or Central examinations!

- Maybe a few handy and dedicated ones amongst you will survive about two decades to initiate a process of Gandhiji's concept of *Ram Rajya* – a real rule of law and moral power!! But it is a long way!!

Sub-Section-6

Mass Entertainment Power

As explained in the Section-I, this facet of power quotents covers a whole sort of areas – music, celebrity shows, reality shows, sports, religious discourses, spiritual dialogues or exercises for mass consumption, etc.

This power is nowhere near the first five described earlier. This depends on all the five. Some may not need crime power much; but will require help in some milder crimes like tax evasion; for getting land, etc. Some people may use some crime-linked persons to win over their competitors. Yes, they also have severe competition from their category of operators: other musicians; other celebrities and celebrity aspirants; other religious leaders, and so on. Yes, everybody will be trying to show that they are the most popular persons or trying to show that they are the most rich and powerful. They need the State power to expand their activities. Also to raise their prestige.

On the other hand politicians require such mass entertainers to attract crowds. See the number of film-stars getting into politics, religious leaders endorsing politicians (blessing), etc.

Money power persons also utilise these mass entertainers very well. They need to keep a good public image.

Crime power wielders also get a lot of benefit from these groups. Those who deal with the religious and spiritual matters for mass entertainment or engagements, have special advantages in a society like India. Therefore, supporting them gives a special social status for which the crime power wielders yearn. And some of them will believe that they will be absolved of "sins" in the other world through their service done in religious fields.

If you want to get into this vast field of entertaining masses of people and rule their hearts (they will be your fans, *bhakta*), then answer for yourself the following questions:

- If you are in this category, you cannot have the status like the powerful politicians, etc. (five levels above). Some of them may also become celebrities and have mass entertaining power. You cannot get that. Still are you aspiring to be in this category to have mass of followers?

- Don't think that since it is low in the rank, it is easy. For the State power, if you pass competitive exams you get into entry level; for crime power one requires very little qualification. Media power is relatively easy compared to say:

  - becoming a reasonably popular film-star,

  - a sportsperson of some standing, etc.,

  - even to become a popular religious/spiritual leader, you need to work hard.

- Do you have an urge to be popular with many people? A big fan crowd?

- Also a situation may arise when you have to suddenly fade away. Your competitors may have taken over or the powerful patrons may have switched over to others!! Though you don't have to think of it in the early stages, but do you have the courage for it? (Of course, this is true for politicians and crime power persons; media persons too! Money power persons may hold on to money even after their peak!!) Then go ahead.

- Are you ready to have a double life (i.e. for the fans you are a great hero, guru, but you depend upon a whole system including other superior powers to maintain your status; you are less powerful than them!).

- Often you cannot make this status as the first goal. You have to become a good musician; actor; sports person; religious master; etc. Then only you can try for this huge fan club. Are you prepared for it?

- Later are you ready to make compromises in your own fields, in order to please the "crowds" and also to "catch hold" of more powerful persons in your fold as patrons. While the fan crowds can be blind followers, the powerful patrons will extract benefits for them!!

- Once you get into this role of mass entertainer, there will be very little of personal life for you – yes, you are driven by the crowds all the days, year after year. Are you ready?

- Also your competitors will throw lots of mud at you; even for things in which you are not involved. Can you develop thick skin? (Of course, all those who aim for power have to develop fairly large thick skin!!)
- You can start anywhere—music, film acting, religion, etc. Keep doing well. Keep an eye on what is popular. How to attract fans? How to replace somebody else?

Sub-Section-7

Emotion Power

A 'democracy' like India does not run just by elections alone. Elections require political power to influence the State power; media power; mass entertainment power, and so on. Even after winning elections with a majority or a patched-up coalition majority, political power in developing countries like India (which practices democracy) does not depend on these constitutional systems alone.

Even decisions taken by a large majority in the Legislative Assembly (of States) or Parliament (at the Centre), cannot be implemented, if a small minority can manage to unleash emotion power in the streets; it may be a minority issue or a religious-emotion, caste or language issue or a protest for land or against an industry or a xenophobia.

It will be very useful, if a deal is struck with media power-holders. Emotions are shortlived. "Breaking news" and repeated video clips and newspaper headlines can keep up the emotion power alive.

In the current "liberal-democratic" milieu, many "nice" issues like human rights, gender issues, poverty, farmer's land, minority religion, etc. are taken up for stoking emotions.

There are many foreign and local sources who will fund such emotion stoking.

The persons who can do such short-term release of emotions into the street can hold political power, in today's coalition politics which may last for two decades more!! You can see it for yourself about the parties and individuals who manage a few Members of Parliament (MPs) or Members of Legislative Assembly (MLAs). They come into limelight on some issues, hold on to stoking emotions through emotional statements and also some violent outburst of emotions in the street such as to come into media and public attention.

Such groups will rarely make it big. Their reach will be limited. But they will have enough nuisance value against the first two (political, money power) and also to those with state power and mass entertainment power-holders. But you can be "darlings" of media for a short while. If you can hold on to such groups to create emotional bursts, you can feel like a leader.

But note one thing: such groups will normally have one autocratic leader. Everything will be done as per her/his whims and fancies. Therefore, if you yourself are not the leader of the group, you will feel terribly repressed.

Sometimes you can get bashed up by bigger groups or between fights of small emotive groups. If you want fierce independence and also power, this is a possible avenue.

Sub-Section-8

Backroom Power

As you would have guessed from the Section-I and much of the Section-II above, there is no rigid watertight compartments between the power-holders; there are also migrations from one to another.

Also most of the power-holders do many things behind the scenes often quite opposite of what they may say in the public. This is a special way of negotiation in a society where hypocrisy is the norm. Often power play in a "civilised" society involves many such hypocrises. This is not particular to India; all around the world, power-players do these tricks. They even strategise these game plays. That is where the role of those who work in the backrooms (without necessarily aspiring for the limelight of leadership) becomes very important. In USA, they openly call them lobbyists; there are companies who offer lobby services just as professional consultants do for technical jobs. Sometimes they overlap with money power and crime power to arrive at accepted negotiations between power players. Many may call themselves think tanks, associations, and academies, etc.

In India we do not openly accept the existence of lobbyists. We tend to hold high moral postures: No intermediaries! No agents! But they do exist in various forms as individuals, institutions (often as NGOs), spiritual/religious leaders, associations, think tanks, assistants in the office of the powerful persons, etc.

Most of those involved in power games know them, watch their movements either to seek their assistance for themselves or nullify their moves to help their enemies!!

These backroom power wielders exist in every field—in all the above seven power hierarchies. Therefore, scope is very high. But you cannot show your power in public!

Are you ready to suppress your own ego like that? Note that you can even make big fellows bend to your ways, but by devious means, by praising them in private and public. Can you sustain it?

You have to be continuously updating your database about likes and dislikes, idiosyncrasies, weaknesses, and movements of those who are powerful and their lieutenants. You have to continually network with them. Be ready to respond to at their beck and call.

Of course, within these backroom power-holders also there are many hierarchies. If you want to rise up you need to do lots of power games within your groups. There will be close friends who will be wanting to stab you (This is true for all the seven power game players!).

But backroom persons' vulnerability is much higher as the competition and enmity within the group is much fierce.

The main power-players themselves often hate their dependence on these backroom persons and try to create conflicts often (as they try to do even within their own loyal staff!!).

But there is fun too! Biggest leaders as seen outside in the public space will beg you to help! You can play one against another!

Sometime it can be frustrating when you are "dumped" by the power-players for your service, or when many of the power-players by your service fall down from power, e.g. political power changes drastically; money power shifts by take-over or fall of companies or State power-holders are changed considerably by new political groups and so on. Clever ones survive by keeping a large network in anticipation.

Entry levels are huge. You can try by entering into lobbying institutions, think tanks, etc. and by yourself developing a network. Help a few fellows as intermediaries. You have to be cautious and not brag. In initial years don't try too much of betrayal politics. Show that you are "trust-worthy"—then you will learn the games. Don't get emotionally attached to any individual/group.

Sub-Section-9

Knowledge Power

As pointed out in the main text, there is a very little scope for knowledge power in India – be it science, technology, literature, arts, philosophy, etc. Most of these persons suffer because they are under the patronage of the state power and therefore political power. Some can try with persons of money power but they really don't need knowledge power. They may have some one as a sycophant to give some aura; then you are not powerful but a slave!!

In science and technology and academic area you can offer some knowledge power. Try for state power, to be Director, Director-General, Vice-Chancellor, Government Secretary, Chairman of top government advisory committees, etc. But here knowledge power does not help. It may be a disadvantage. One requires "tribal" affiliation to the old persons hierarchies which have set in during the past sixty years. It is difficult to dislodge them; even if they die at very old age, their "tribal" choices are waiting in the wings.

Only where knowledge power can have some scope is in the area of clinical medicines and surgery. Even here after entry you have to suffer a hierarchy for about one-and-half decade before you can emerge on your own!

If you want to be just pursuing knowledge without other power politics given above, you are really not a power seeker! You may have an ego to be known as a great person in your narrow selected field. Such a possibility and opportunities exist in the developed world. There are some biases and glass ceilings. But by and large you can pursue your work. If you aim at very high awards like Nobel Prize, Pulitzer Prize and other such prestigious awards, keep in mind there are severe power politics!

Sub-Section-10

Moral Power

There are very few persons – miniscule in number – who have moral power. They can live up to the high principles of civilised society. They are not to be judged by external forms: "simple", "very loving to all", "soft spoken", etc. Vicious power-players use many of these garbs including usage of many "holy symbols" of religions.

Those who fit in for a true description of moral power, will be like as per the description of Guru Govind Singh in "Chaubis Avtar" reproduced below:

> "They all deceived the people with their dress and form, but, the Saints advertise themselves not, yea, they who lean only on the name of God,
>
> Man stages many false shows to earn bread;
>
> For, he attains the riches of the world in no wise else;
>
> But, he who dwells on the One God alone,
> He practices no such deceits; he believes in the One."

Guru Govind Singh,
In "Chaubis Avtar"

I have not added this moral power into Table-1 for marking.

Some of you after getting fed up with various forms of power play may ultimately aspire to reach this stage and some way succeed too! God bless you!

7

How to Assess Your Power Quotient (PQ)

Now you come to the most important section in this book which will help you decide which path you will take.

But do not rush to fill up the Table-1 on the next page. After carefully studying Section-I and Section-II, think about it yourself. You will have a very few people with whom you can discuss as you will have to reveal your true inner secrets to the persons whose advice you seek. Therefore, you have to be alone in your decision making. Be truthful to yourself and check your power quotient (PQ).

If you consult others, ask these questions to yourself. Is the person reliable? Can you trust him/her? How long? Will the person go against you after several years if not right away? Well, there are risks. All power games are risky! Also only high risks bring high rewards if you succeed! (an untold thing is that high damage also if you fail!).

If you don't consult anybody you will not have the benefit of better knowledge. You may be getting trapped in your own (ill-conceived) fantasies or fears! On the other hand too much exposure can make you vulnerable; your ideas may leak to others who are keen on creating problems for you.

Table-1: Selecting Your Priority

Sl. No.	Nature of Power	Depth of your desire	Your overall situation and enabling conditions progress	Your under-standing of the process at entry point and further assessment of your ability	Your attitude towards others in the field and your own	Commitment to do a long haul through failures and difficulties
1.	Political					
2.	Money					
3.	Crime					
4.	Media					
5.	State					
6.	Mass Entertainment					
7.	Emotion					
8.	Backroom					
9.	Knowledge					

Table-2: Results of Markings

Sl. No.	Power in order of selection	Marks
1		
2		
3		
4		
5		
6		
7		
8		
9		

So judge the risks that your PQ may invite! That pain of decision making is your first step in climbing up a power ladder.

Then note down important points: strengths, weaknesses, opportunities, threats and pros and cons.

Analysis helps to take better decisions in conformity with your PQ, but too much of it can lead into paralysis in action.

So, learn to balance these two. Pain of such balancing is yours. This is the second step in the power ladder.

No more suspense or tension. Go to the Table-1 given in the beginning of this Chapter.

Political Power

After all the above study and two steps, take a deep breath, release the breath slowly. Repeat it a few times. Calm your mind, probably thinking something good and nice in your life.

Step (I): With that calmness, go to Row-1, Column-1 and ask yourselves what is the depth of your desire for the item number one, i.e. political power. Rate it in a scale of ten:

Extremely High	10 or 9
Very-very high	8 or 7
Very high	6 or 5
High	4 or 3
Fair	2
Poor	1

Step (II): If you arrive at number 9 or 10 or 3 or 1, ask yourself again, whether you are being truthful to yourself. Am I cheating myself? Or am I truthful? You will get an answer. Whatever number you get as inner statement that you are truthful, put that number in Column-1, Row-1.

Preferably write in ink; otherwise you may have a temptation to vacillate by erasing the pencil mark. Even if you change the ink mark it will stare at you! If you change many times, it means you are confused! You have to restart some other day or time when you are calm. But following the Steps (I) and (II) as indicated above.

Step (III): Having marked in the Column-1 for the item of first row, go to Column-2 for first row, i.e. for political power. What is your assessment of overall situation and enabling conditions? What does it mean? How is your personal life? Do you think the political parties as they exist around attract you to start a process? You may be in a metro or in a small town, does not matter. Do you feel strongly that there is something you can contribute to some of the party or a political leader by making a beginning? If you have started on an experimental basis, do you assess that you can now make it more permanent? Say to increase the time period and days of involvement or full time? Do you feel that conditions are good? Think about these calmly to get a general idea. If you think you are reasonably clear about it, then get to Step (IV).

Step (IV): Essentially it is the same as Step (II) in terms of marking. The general ideas you had (have) from Step (III) above have to be captured in a number between 1 to 10. Rankings are the same. All items said in Step (II) apply in terms of your finally making an ink mark. Also restart question in case your markings are vacillating too much. But firm up your mind to avoid remembering all what you have thought of. You have so many steps to go. Therefore, take courage to decide. Give a clear marking.

Then go to the Step (V). You would have yourself found out what it is. That is for political power (Row-1). Look at Column-3, i.e. what is your understanding of the processes at the entry point and further on to progress. That is after assessing your deep desire in Column-1 and then the overall situation in Column-2, you are now looking at some detailed processes as to how you can start your march towards power for this Row-1.

Step (V): Assess Row-1 for Column-3. Do you know whom to approach to enter into political career? Some reasonable understanding of the person (s) whom you have to contact? Yes, these are the nitty-gritty details of entry. Not all the power ladders have equal type of entry. For state power you have All India entrance tests such as IAS, etc; for media power there are courses you take and enter into one newspaper, TV, and other mass media. For some areas like political there are no application forms, no minimum marks, and such other things! Do you know which party or group you will enter? Part time or full time? How will you move on further? You should have done your own "research" around your area before you venture to mark in the table.

Again there are dilemmas such as whether to enter into big party or a small one. For a small one the entry may be easy; but overall size of the party may remain same for years! However, it can give you training. In big parties, there may be many entry barriers. If you don't have good connections, you may start at a very low level and further going up may be difficult.

Yes, you have to think of all problems and opportunities at the entry point and further progress (yes, it is a guess, but all the same you have to mentally go through it!). Yes, prepare your mind to make the marking from 1 to 10. Yes, remove the anxieties whether you are going to undermark or over mark. Don't think of the earlier two markings. This is true of all the steps you are going to go through. Yes, you have to think carefully. There is nothing called the ultimate answer. You have to learn to make the best of judgement under such uncertain (and anxious, because it involves you!) circumstances. If you learn it, you can master your power games as well!

Step (VI): Yes, having prepared yourself in Step (V), get into the Step (VI). Basically it is like Steps (II) and (IV). You have to mark 1 to 10. The gradation is as in Step (III). Make yourself calm as explained in Steps (II) and (IV)and mark for Column-3 opposite Row-1.

Step (VII): Then shift your attention to Row-1 Column-4 "Your attitude towards others in the field and your own assessment of your ability". Note the important differences from the earlier three. (These will apply to all other Rows as well).

Column-1 was depth of desire. How much you feel? Something like your "inner call".

Column-2 was a macro parameter. Overall situation and enabling conditions (as you judge it). Here you have cut off yourself from your deep desire and analysing the situation more rationally and objectively.

Column-3 refers to the nitty-gritty of operational plans. How to enter, pros and cons of different options available for entry, processes for further progress, etc. That is from macro assessment of situation, you are considering some details of how to...? Macro assessment and these details need not always tally.

Column-4: Again you are coming back to assess yourself: not just your desire, your knowledge about details of processes of entry and further progress, but your own attitude towards others in the field and your own assessment to work. Yes, this is an assessment by yourself as to how good you are, to work in a team and also as to how you can manage a team? If you have contempt for everybody in a group you are going to join, it is unlikely you can function well (will you have to choose some other groups!). If you are afraid of or in too much admiration of many persons, then also you are likely to be pushed down; you cannot then rise up in the system. In a way, it is an integrated view about your functioning after having made your thoughts on items on Columns 2 and 3 for Row-1. Your assessment of Column-4, implicitly takes into account your ideas for items in Columns 2 and 3 for the row concerned. Now you do Row-1 Column-4 (you will do so for other rows also similarly for these columns).

Step (VII) consists of such an assessment by you—the pros and cons, the contradictions, weaknesses, strengths, opportunities and challenges. Assess how you are likely to function.

Step (VIII): Then go to Step (VIII) using all the precautions and methodologies for the Steps (II), (IV) and (VI) mark between 1 to 10 for Step (VIII).

Column-5: Then go to Step (IX), i.e. Column-5 for Row-1. This is your assessment about your own commitment to do a long haul through successes and failures. For coming to Step (IX) Column-5 you have gone through intensely earlier eight Steps fully concentrating on Row-1, Political Power: Your desire, overall macro situation, the nitty-gritty of entry processes and your own abilities in a team, etc. Now your mind has to switch gears and look at the future. What is your commitment to do a long haul through many failures and difficulties? All what you have thought of earlier, have to come before you as an integrated whole and then you project yourself into the future. Can you sustain for two or three decades? That is the crucial question you have to answer honestly to yourself. It is not an interview with somebody who is going to recruit you! It is an answer which will truthfully decide your future. If you are truthful to yourself, then chances of your successes are very high.

Are you mentally ready to assess yourself, then enter Step (X). Mark between 1 to 10 depending upon how you assess your long-term commitment level.

Put that number. Now don't try to add the total. Don't look back any of the five numbers.

Money Power

Go to Row-2. Don't say I have made up my mind. Good to go through all the nine rows and all their associated columns. Revisit Step (I) to (X) for each of the Row.

Step (XI): For Row-2 and Column-1. Again you have to revisit Step (I) for Row-2, i.e. your desire to acquire money power. Remember all what is told in Step (I), when ready then go to Step (XII).

Step (XII) is again the repeat of Step (II) but for money power. Then mark between 1 to 10 what exactly you feel.

Step (XIII): This is Row-2, money power for Column-2. All those considerations as given in Step (III) have to be done by you for money power.

When you are ready to mark, go to Step (XIV), you will have to repeat all the items of Step (IV) in the context of you and money power. Mark between 1 to 10.

Step (XV): You would have already learnt the drill. Row-2 Column-3 similar considerations as in Step (V) but in the context of money power of Row-2.

Step (XVI): Marking between 1 to 10. Similar considerations as for Step (VI) decide and then mark.

Then Row-2, Column-4.

Step (XVII). Considerations similar to Step (VII).

Step (XVIII) Considerations similar to Step (VIII). Mark.

Then Row-2, Column-5. Similar way.

Step (XIX) as in Step (IX).

Step (XX) as in Step (X).

Again don't add total for row.

Now you are the master for other Rows & Columns.

Crime Power

Go to Row-3

Row-3 Column-1

Step (XXI) as in Step (I)

Step (XXII) as in Step (II)

Row-3 Column-2

Step (XXIII) as in Step (III)

Step (XXIV) as in Step (IV)

I think you are smart enough.

You will go Column-3 two Steps as (V) & (VI)

Column-4 as in (VII), (VIII)

Column-5 as in (IX), (X)

You have reached Step (XXX), i.e. Step -30

Don't add.

Each Row has two steps per each column. Thus has 10 steps.

Media Power

So then you go to Row-4 (Media).

You will go from Step (XXXI) (31) and reach Step (XXXX) (40)

Considerations are similar;

Column-1 as in Step (I) & (II)

Column-2 as in Step (III) & (IV)

Column-3 as in Step (V) & (VI)

Column-4 as in Step (VII) & (VIII)

Column-5 as in Step (IX) & (X)

Steps (I), (III), (V), (VII) & (IX) are thinking steps.

Step (II), (IV), (VI), (VII) & (X) are marking steps.

For the last 9th Row (knowledge power), you will reach 90th step. You repeat these processes and markings for all the rows: state power, Row-5; mass entertainment power, Row-6; emotion power, Row-7 and backroom power, Row-8. When you reach the last step, i.e. Row-9, Column-5 second step (90th), then relax and take deep breath for a few times preferably closing your eyes.

Results of Your Markings

Then open up your eyes.

Add the numbers you have marked for each of the rows. Now you have ranked yourself for each of the power structure.

Results may surprise you. Take a sheet of paper and write down the top one first – its name (Political, Money, etc.) and total marks a in Table-2.

Keep looking at it. Check the differences between the first three in the serial number. If it is very small say between 1 & 2 only 3 marks; 2 & 3 is only within 3 marks.

If the differences are 5 marks or above then your choices are clear. Difference 4 is marginal; if the differences are 3 & below, you need to repeat.

You can ignore all items in Table-2 beyond serial 4, unless of course, your differences are only 1, 1 only. In such narrow cases I suggest that you see for the difference between the top of the serial and the one which is clearly 10 marks below. Say your Sl. No. of Table-2 is 40 marks. You have to look for the marks 30. Suppose 30 marks occur at Sl. No. 6 of your Table-2, then you have to repeat all the 5 (one above the 10 marks difference). If 10 marks difference is say at Sl. 4, then you have to take only up to Sl. No. 1, 2, 3.

If it happens say at Sl. 8, something is wrong with your markings – your thinking! You are wanting everything!! Means you will get nothing! Anyway, repeat the exercise based on the above principle – not immediately, but giving at least one hour gap. If possible eat something which you like well, nap and restart the whole exercise from Step (I) to the end 90.

But when it is only 4 or five items, restart the marking only for those rows. Repeat it to a point when the Table-2 you arrive at a clear difference of minimum 5 marks between the top Sl. No. 1 of your new Table-2 and the Sl. No. 2.

Then Sl. No. 1 of Table-2 is the choice with which you should choose your career with an option of Sl. No. 2, the final Table-2 as a mid-course corrections in your life.

Those of you who achieve a clear difference in Sl. No. 1, 2, 3 at the beginning itself more than 5, you need to be applauded as you are clear-headed about yourself and probably truthful too!

Good luck!

For those who have to repeat once, I have no special advice. You proceed on the same lines as above.

For those who have to repeat more than twice, I suggest you take a break of a day or two, relax and then restart.

Now you may wonder how accurate these are, to give results in actual life. Please note that all these items are very complex and many judgements are involved especially related to you.

The methods suggested here are based on many intuitive judgements and experience. They are more meant to imbibe some discipline in your thinking processes and enhance your power quotient (PQ).

The details explained in Steps (I) to (X) are meant to challenge you and to make you cautious. It has been suggested that you arrive at clear differences in marking because it helps to clarify your priorities. If you find the marking surprising to you, then ask your mind calmly whether you are right or not. Search your mind whether anything went wrong seriously when you mark.

Your mind is the truthful authority. Most likely you will arrive at it. If you want to change your choices, after such an examination, even against the markings in the serial nos. in Table-2 you have finally arrived at, do so after questioning yourself vigorously. After all whatever be the process, you have to live with your own decision. The entire exercise was/ is meant to prepare you for your choices.

Finally, choose a path, remember what is told in Section I, and start your march to identify your existing PQ and also understand how to increase it.

Pray to God, if you are a believer.

Keep repeat readings of this book once a year at least.

I wish you all the best!